Igniting Wonder, Reflection, and Change in Our Schools

Containing real stories from real school leaders, teachers, students, and parents in seven key areas, this book demonstrates how educators can use narrative to trigger wonder, reflection, and change in their classrooms and schools. By including real examples of the narrative process in action, this book invites educators to think deeply about their daily practices, struggles, and victories in order to carry out immediate and incredible changes in their own schools. The authentic stories presented in this book offer ideas for fostering a positive learning environment and for finding solutions to the most challenging issues they face today in areas such as teacher–student relationships, learning and instruction, assessment, motivation, educational policies and politics, and student engagement. By using the powerful self-reflective tool of narrative, this book will help educators to increase student achievement while constructing a positive school culture that is built on igniting authentic stories.

Rick Jetter is an Educational Consultant for K–12 schools across the nation and a speaker, trainer, and multi-genre author. He has worked in the field of education as a teacher, assistant principal, principal, assistant superintendent, and superintendent of schools.

Other Eye On Education Books
Available from Routledge
(www.routledge.com/eyeoneducation)

Hiring the Best Staff for Your School: How to Use Narrative to Improve Your Recruiting Process
Rick Jetter

Keeping the Leadership in Instructional Leadership: Developing Your Practice
Linda L. Carrier

The Educational Leader's Guide for School Scheduling: Strategies Addressing Grades K–12
Elliot Y. Merenbloom and Barbara A. Kalina

A Road Map to PLC Success
Sean McWherter

Leadership in America's Best Urban Schools
Joseph F. Johnson, Jr, Cynthia L. Uline, and Lynne G. Perez

Leading Learning for ELL Students: Strategies for Success
Catherine Beck and Heidi Pace

Leadership in Americas Best Urban Schools
Joseph F. Johnson, Jr, Cynthia L. Uline, and Lynne G. Perez

Ten Steps for Genuine Leadership in Schools
David M. Fultz

The Power of Conversation: Transforming Principals into Great Leaders
Barbara Kohm

First Aid for Teacher Burnout: How You Can Find Peace and Success
Jenny G. Rankin

What Successful Principals Do! 199 Tips for Principals, Second Edition
Franzy Fleck

The Revitalized Tutoring Center: A Guide to Transforming School Culture
Jeremy Koselak and Brad Lyall

7 Ways to Transform the Lives of Wounded Students
Joe Hendershott

Igniting Wonder, Reflection, and Change in Our Schools

An Educator's Guide to Using Authentic Stories

Rick Jetter

Routledge
Taylor & Francis Group
NEW YORK AND LONDON

First published 2017
by Routledge
711 Third Avenue, New York, NY 10017

and by Routledge
2 Park Square, Milton Park, Abingdon, Oxon, OX14 4RN

Routledge is an imprint of the Taylor & Francis Group, an informa business

© 2017 Taylor & Francis

The right of Rick Jetter to be identified as the author of this work has been asserted by him in accordance with sections 77 and 78 of the Copyright, Designs and Patents Act 1988.

All rights reserved. No part of this book may be reprinted or reproduced or utilised in any form or by any electronic, mechanical, or other means, now known or hereafter invented, including photocopying and recording, or in any information storage or retrieval system, without permission in writing from the publishers.

Trademark notice: Product or corporate names may be trademarks or registered trademarks, and are used only for identification and explanation without intent to infringe.

Library of Congress Cataloging-in-Publication Data
A catalog record for this book has been requested

ISBN: 978-1-138-22059-1 (hbk)
ISBN: 978-1-138-22060-7 (pbk)
ISBN: 978-1-315-41249-8 (ebk)

Typeset in Optima
by Apex CoVantage, LLC

To all of the amazing educators out there who believe that stories are the best kind of research and who believe that references, works cited lists, or bibliographies are subordinate to what you experience each day while working with students and colleagues. Your own stories do not need reference sections or tables and diagrams. Just tell it like it is!

Play with stories, not matches.

P.S. I did use some references within my bibliographies, but not to create or theorize new knowledge. Stories can take care of that!

Contents

Meet the Author ix
Preface xi
Acknowledgments xvii

1. **When and How to Constructively Use Authentic Stories at Your School**   1
   Stories as Social Legacies   3
   The Top Seven Areas of Powerful Storytelling   5
   How to Use Stories   8
   When to Use Stories   14

2. **Stories that Improve and IGNITE School, Community, and Interpersonal Relationships**   18
   Strengthening Teacher–Student Relationships   18
   Strengthening Staff–Staff Relationships   25
   Strengthening Educator–Parent and Community Relationships   29

3. **Stories that IGNITE Powerful Instruction with Reduced Variance**   31
   Instruction   32
   Digital Blindness   33
   Teaching "Responsibility"   37
   The Power of Feedback   41
   The Redundant Curriculum   44
   Fieldtrips and Recess   45

Contents

4. **Stories that IGNITE Advocacy for Thoughtful Assessment** 50
    Homework and Pop Quizzes, One Century Later 51
    "Pop" Goes the Pop Quizzes 54
    Popsicle Sticks 56
    Writing Portfolios 58
    Test Construction and Preparation 60

5. **Stories that Make Us Wonder about Our Own Policies** 64
    Policies that are Silly 65
    Policies that are Missing 66
    Policies that Leverage 68
    Policies that are Abused or Taken for Granted 70
    Policies that Protect 71

6. **Stories that Help Us to Work through Educational Politics** 75
    Common Core Politics 75
    The Common Core State Standards and "New" Math 78
    The Opt-Out Movement and High-Stakes Tests 80
    Follow the Leader through the Chain of Command? 81
    Questioning Decision Making 83
    The Race for a School Board Seat 85

7. **Stories that IGNITE and Motivate Teachers and School Leaders** 89
    Stories of Victory 90
    Stories of Defeat 94
    Recognizing the Conditions for Celebrating Educators 97

8. **Stories Written by Students for Helping Other Students or Adults** 99
    Teaching Narrative Writing 100
    Boys Will Be Boys? 101
    Posting Student Work (a Story in Reverse)? 101
    The Never-Ending Discipline Cycle? 102
    What about My IEP? Creating Students with Voice 103
    Master Schedules from a Student's Perspective? 104

Meet the Author

Dr. Rick Jetter (a.k.a. Dr. J.) is an educational consultant for K–12 schools across the nation and a multi-genre author. He is one of a small group of thought leaders who work in the field of narrative theory research for improving public, private, charter, and community schools for our students.

Deeply involved in narrative theory research, this is Rick's third book related to using narrative theory as a practical methodology for improving every facet of education. His other narrative theory books include the following: *Escaping the School Leader's Dunk Tank: How to Prevail When Others Want to See You Drown* (Dave Burgess Consulting, LLC, 2016, with Rebecca Coda) and *Hiring the Best Staff for Your School: How to Use Narrative to Improve Your Recruiting Process* (Routledge, 2016). Rick is also working on his fourth narrative theory book, titled *Stories from the Playground: How Students Use Narratives to Help Adults Solve REAL Problems in Schools*. His sixth manuscript, titled *The Internet of Things: Connecting Education to a Global Revolution*, and seventh manuscript, titled *Brain Scars: Bullying, Neuroscience, and the Law*, are also forthcoming.

Rick is also the author of a mysterious and powerful middle-grades novel about autism and bullying, titled *The Isolate /n./* (Motivational Press, 2016), and a book about the power of using mindfulness in your daily life, titled *Sutures of the Mind* (Motivational Press, 2015).

Rick has worked in the field of education for over 18 years. He started his career as an alternative education teacher before becoming a middle school English teacher. He has held public school leadership positions as a middle school assistant principal, elementary school principal, assistant superintendent, and superintendent of schools before pursuing a career of educational consulting, speaking, writing, and publishing. Rick also serves the educational community as the Director of K–12 Education for

Meet the Author

Advanced Educational Products (AEP) in New York State and is a weekly featured columnist with Rebecca Coda for *School Leaders Now*.

Rick even coaches writers and authors across various industries, including education, the health/sciences, the humanities, and the business industry. His other books, speaking engagement topics, and training sessions can be found by visiting www.rickjetter.com and www.rjconsultants.org for his consulting services. You may also contact Rick directly at drjetter1@gmail.com.

Bring IGNITE to Your School!

Rick has been working with schools across the nation on professional development initiatives focused on narratives and school reform through storytelling. His latest presentation at the NCTE 2016 National Conference in Atlanta, Georgia, highlighted what Rick can bring to your school. Topics vary, according to needs, but can include any of the following areas:

- School leadership and teacher leadership for surviving the "dunk tank"
- Best practices for hiring staff
- Mindfulness in the classroom
- Using stories in classrooms and schools to IGNITE change and much, much more!

# Preface

Stories have been around for as long as life itself has existed. But sometimes, stories get a bad rap. They end up being used for comedic, entertainment purposes or punchlines to some very bad jokes. But, then, our elders tell stories about the war or growing up, perhaps, and that is a *good* thing. Stories, like this, reflect history beyond textbooks. A spouse might tell us stories about how his or her day went. Maybe we listen to them, or maybe we zone out – not because we don't love them, but because our head is reeling with our own day, our own stories.

We hear all sorts of stories from our children, and sometimes, we decide what is important by *tuning in* or *turning off* the good jelly inside the jelly donut nestled inside someone else's story. Sometimes we yawn hearing others' stories. Sometimes, stories make us sit on the edge of our seats. Sometimes stories are used to teach us about a topic or to help us learn something . . . anything. Stories can also *heal* us.

Often times, stories are forgotten – whether we forget to tell someone something or fail to tell it "back" to someone else. Sometimes, we forget to document or record a story, and we wish that we captured a particular story about a moment in our lives for others to experience. We gather wisdom each day, but so do our students. Have we captured their stories and archived them for our own learning or for our own consumption to use for improving classrooms and schools everywhere? Have we captured the stories of our colleagues – you know, even those football field bleacher stories or the parking lot stories that are not always gossipy? We have ideas. We generate solutions even when we are not formally sitting at a desk or standing up in front of a classroom. We think about ways to improve instruction, but all we have at the end of the day are forgotten stories that could have helped us tackle something. Solve something. Unless we archive our

Preface

moments, they will slip by us. That's the exact point in time where a story becomes a narrative. A written narrative. Archived, forever, good or bad. It becomes part of our educational footprint for others to consider.

Whatever the case may be, stories are catching on again in the field of education. If anything, I'm trying to IGNITE stories everywhere so it gathers more combustion for educators and students. Some of my colleagues are also igniting stories everywhere. It is a form of research like no other. You don't need graphs, charts, statistical analysis using SPSS, or any other form of data crunching other than a story, itself, as you start to wonder, reflect, or change what you can do *right now* about something that someone has talked about or shared with you – those thoughts from the field with heart.

There's no doubt about it, though. Stories are everywhere. And, they are being written and shared by students, parents, teachers, board of education members, school and district leaders, and you and me. We all love a good story. C'mon. You know you do. Sometimes the stories we see in print, online, on TV, or hear on the radio help us to wonder, reflect, or get fired up about *something* that we are passionate about changing – all for the sake of helping our educational community learn and grow.

Better yet: stories are also strategic tools to advocate for what is just or right in education, and powerful stories can carve new identities into our souls, transform us into something new, or simply help us to reflect and refract within our own professional social constructs and circles. We wonder why something happens, prepare for what might come, and think about how to do something even better than we did before as we canvas our *told stories* and sort through the major plotlines that will pack a punch in our profession because we receive a call to action on a topic that we can relate to.

We have been taught to show, not tell; demonstrate, not lecture; and place our hands in the muddy core of the earth to feel the worms, rather than only read about them in books. We *connect* with stories. They make *issues* come alive. Stories are the worms that we should feel between our fingers. They are *real* and they are, sometimes, muddy too. But, they help us grow, learn, and respect the human spirit. Our experiences are projected into the stories we tell, and as a result, stories are serious accounts of what we feel are important morsels of life. We take them seriously because they are authentic, packed with emotions, packed with fervor and feelings, and act as representations of who we are within a particular snapshot in time. Our identity-in-the-making grabs hold of stories and wrestles with them as it might transform us into a more purposeful or knowledgeable professional.

Better yet, when we encounter stories that we hear, and they are not transcribed in some way, the power of *narrativizing* our stories creates a time capsule for us, always and forever. As I said earlier, narratives are permanent fixtures even though we are constantly being transformed in so many different ways while reading stories that have been documented for our eyes. When our stories are put in writing, they tickle our senses through our eyes and they become concrete examples of the verbal stories which might be forgotten. That's the research that is captured. It is astonishing!

For principals and teachers, students' stories can be archived to achieve greater things in the classrooms and schools of today and tomorrow. Written stories galvanize emotion, and emotions make us wonder and reflect about everything going on around us. Stories advocate for our voices which we don't want to lose. They bring real, tangible hearts and souls to the discussion table, and it is difficult to discount the stories that we share with one another – the written ones that are placed right in front of our noses. Stories *breathe* like we do. That is a different concept, isn't it? Speaking of *different* . . .

What is Different about this Book?

Igniting Wonder, Reflection, and Change in Our Schools will do just what it says: IGNITE you with REAL stories that will promote positive change in our schools or just simply make you wonder about something as you kick a topic or idea around in your head. That's innovation. Stories will help you to reflect on making your leadership or instruction better for your students. Stories will also strengthen your relationships with your colleagues and students too. Stories IGNITE us!

This book will teach you how to use stories within the educational system, provide examples of when it is appropriate to use them, contextually, and offer you dozens and dozens of examples of how you can use stories to foster amazing learning cultures in your schools when voices are placed at the forefront and used as tools to IGNITE wonder, reflection, and positive change. This book will advocate for the powerful voices of various stakeholders who have an interest in child development, teaching, leading, and learning. There are very few books for educators which demonstrate

Preface

how narrative theory can be used within school-wide contexts for improving culture, academics, community, and relationships. I've devoted my entire career in education to narrative theory and by documenting stories in print. That is my contribution to creating an educational reform time capsule. This book provides loads of authentic stories that can be used in your school, starting RIGHT NOW.

Who was this Book Written for?

Teachers and school leaders stand at the front doors of their classrooms and schools. This book is for you. School district leaders who hold the keys to all of their buildings will also love this book. But, wait: parents will *also* love this book. If you are a parent who just simply wants to know more about how stories can help schools, grab a copy and then pass it off to a teacher or, better yet, place a copy in their mailbox with one of your own stories attached to it so that they can start to wonder and reflect about the wisdom that you have and what you know about schools and raising children.

How will this Book be Useful to You?

People ask me the following question all the time: what can stories do for *me*? This book can be useful for you in three major ways:

1. You will understand the **appropriate contexts** for using stories to trigger wonder, reflection, and change opportunities within your schools. Yes, there are times when stories or the anonymity of the writer need to be protected. There are times when names shouldn't be named. This book will offer practical advice on how to professionally use stories without causing any harm, conflict, or trouble within your organization. Remember, professionals should be able to get anything off their chest, but not at the risk of being ostracized or looked upon as a "Mr. or Miss-know-it-all."

2. You will learn how **stories can IGNITE people** even when a topic, challenge, or problem is boring, uninspiring, or just plain ridiculous, in

your opinion. You will see how stories can lift up any lifeless corpse of an issue and tackle the daily minutia that we all feel in our career realities in education at one time or another. Stories can resuscitate situations, problems, or challenges when there is no breath left. And, who wants to feel breathless?

3. You will be able to start **transcribing your own authentic told stories** right now and put them to use, immediately, within your school as you tackle problems or offer insights into anything ranging from student–teacher relationships to instruction to assessments to politics or to anything else that schools deal with, day in and day out. Students can start writing their own narratives to help other students too. Teachers can write narratives to help their students out with something that they are struggling with in the classroom. School leaders can utilize stories to capture the attention of their parents or school board members. Superintendents can help others live through story crafting and get us back to a time when human education trumps test-driven education.

This book is organized to include some of the most popular topical areas where stories will IGNITE and can leverage positive changes within a school or district. Chapter 1 will provide a smorgasbord of stories within various categories for educators to consider, but it will do something more than that: it will help you to understand the proper context (time and place) for using narratives in your organization. Chapter 2 will provide stories that focus on building positive relationships at your school. This is one of my favorite chapters because everything; absolutely *everything* in education, either succeeds or fails because of our human relationships. Chapter 3 will focus on instruction and reducing variance at your school. Variance is the enemy of achieving widespread quality and, as educators, we should be creating consistent, replicable, high-quality learning situations for *all* students without turning ourselves over to the "robot army." Chapter 4 will provide insights about authentic assessment through the eyes of those who desire growth outside of the summative assessment environment that is being pushed forth so hard right now, especially when state-driven high-stakes tests provide us with data that come to us too late in the game. Chapter 5 will shine a light on our own policy construction or what we need to stop doing "because we have always done it that way." Chapter 6 will confront a few issues regarding local and national politics and demonstrate how stories can bring about passionate solutions for our students, teachers, and school leaders who do not want politics to stand in the way of student progress. Chapter 7 will include stories that will lift up teachers and school leaders and make them feel good about all of the wonderful things that they do for children each day. Finally, Chapter 8 will provide a few examples about how students write stories for other students to help their classmates learn and grow in amazing ways. Students' stories can also help the adults in our schools to solve real problems in our classrooms and schools, as well.

First, offering insights into the appropriate contexts of how and when we can use stories to strengthen our schools is the rational place to start because there are *right* (appropriate) times to use stories within school settings, and there are *wrong* (inappropriate) times to use stories. There just are.

What will you do to IGNITE your organization? What stories will you tell to trigger necessary changes in the system?

Disclaimer: *For the stories and testimonies within this book, both fictitious names and locations have been used to protect the rights and anonymity of those who participated in sharing their stories for this book. Any similarities in real-life names, titles, or locations are, merely, the result of coincidence.*

Acknowledgments

It's just amazing how many people have contacted me to share a story in the field of education that not only compelled them, but also lead to some sort of wonder, reflection, or positive change in their classrooms or schools. In 2010, I started using narrative theory research as it pertained to how principals responded to narratives to navigate through a high-stakes testing culture of accountability. Back then, this was a groundbreaking topic because the school leaders who participated in my research provided incredible insights for so many different policy decision-makers and grassroots stakeholder groups who were opposed to high-stakes testing. High-stakes tests have been beaten up, left and right, along the way, as the opt-out movement has positioned parents to be heard throughout all levels of local and federal governance. It was because of our stories that the beatings on high-stakes tests occurred.

Since then, I have conducted narrative theory research for enhancing talent searches and hiring practices for recruiting and acquiring the best school staff possible (Jetter, 2016), and now this book reports the newest narrative theory research as it pertains to igniting wonder, reflection, and change in our classrooms and schools of today.

I'm already planning a third book for this series, titled *Stories from the Playground: How Students Use Narratives to Help Educators Solve REAL Problems in Schools*, and I cannot wait to share it with you. It highlights the power of students' narratives in helping others as they strive to make their own schools even better. It positions students as problem solvers, not subordinate subjects where adults make all the decisions because we think we know them better than they know themselves. Chapter 8 in *IGNITE* will give you a taste of the power of student stories.

Acknowledgments

I would like thank all of the educators who have contributed their stories to the growing bank of narratives that can be used to carry out further narrative theory research. I know that your contributions will resonate with readers and compel them to utilize authentic stories, themselves, as a catapult for solving problems, offering opportunities for personal and professional reflection, or, merely, to cause reform or change that will help students in schools throughout the nation. Stories can tug at your heart, spark emotion, and even help to solve the smallest problem. Our voices, reflected through our stories, should be afforded the chance to be heard. That is the essence behind the framework of narrative theory and the power given to this book by educators everywhere.

Finally, this book was written for my children, Edward, Honora, and Ellen, in hopes that they tell their stories to as many people as possible to help, heal, or motivate someone else to be the best that they can be, inside or outside the classroom.

Reference

Jetter, R. (2016). *Hiring the best staff for your school: How to use narrative to improve your recruiting process.* New York: Routledge.

When and How to Constructively Use Authentic Stories at Your School

It would be silly for me to say that there are stories that *matter* and stories that *don't really matter*, but the premise of this chapter is to establish the types of stories that can have the greatest impact on your school and then help you to navigate through when and how to use them for building wonder, reflection, and change in your school.

If you are wondering about how stories can help you to wonder, then this is the type of reflection that this chapter will help to elicit. Imagine this: you are talking to a parent about a bullying situation, and instead of just telling a parent that everything is going to be okay, you actually tell a story of a similar student situation where various strategies helped to deal with a bully. Not using the *actual* students' names, you portray a situation something like this to a parent you are talking to on the phone about his or her own child being bullied in a similar fashion as depicted below:

> *Last year, Timothy had a problem on the playground with Ariana, and when I met and chatted with Timothy, he didn't know how to handle Ariana's name calling every single day. Timothy looked defeated. His face was sullen. He looked like he'd had enough. Second graders can be taught how to advocate for themselves just like any other child in any other grade. So, a few days later, Timothy had the confidence to walk up to Ariana before lunch and hand her a small Zip Lock bag of Goldfish crackers. He said to Ariana, "Since we are friends, I brought this in for you today so we could eat them in lunch together. I mean, if you would sit with me." Ariana looked at Timothy with confusion in her eyes. She didn't know what to say at first. She never expected*

When and How to Use Authentic Stories

> Timothy to be nice to her. After all, she'd been picking on him since the start of school and he thought that they were friends? Well, Ariana gently took the crackers, awkwardly smiled, and ended up eating lunch with Timothy and four of his friends that day. I'm not saying that this is going to work for your child, but Timothy's situation is almost exactly like your son's situation, and I'd like to put our heads together to come up with ideas that your son can use, proactively, just like this.
>
> – Miss Gleason, second-grade teacher

Stories do more than just assure or reassure even the most skeptical skeptic out there. But, one thing is for sure: a story told is better than not telling a story at all. Stories add spice to the bland tomato sauce. Stories can tug emotions for educators, parents, and students. Real examples from real students transform school cultures, and there is always a contextual outlet for you to share a story with someone else for assisting with your school culture. It may take a little longer than simply reassuring someone of something in a few simple sentences, but the lasting effects can be incredible.

Here, Miss Gleason did not use the names of the real children who were involved in a similar bullying episode, but she rather thought about the role that confidentiality plays in her daily life as a teacher. She wasn't hasty or haphazard, but instead, she was very calculated and proper.

- **Wonder**: What was the outcome of the impact and influence of this story on the parent and child who needed assistance with a bully?
- **Reflection**: What kinds of stories can you think of right now in any kind of situation that could help someone else to figure out some new way of thinking or handling of a problem?
- **Change**: Keep confidentiality at the forefront of your story sharing and narrative construction designs. There is a right time to share stories and then there are story violations that will send you in to a boiling pot of water.

So, how else might educators look at areas of programming, human relations, or systematic structures to bring about all sorts of positive changes for their organizations? Here are a few things to keep in mind as you consider increasing your story repertoire for helping everyone in any position within your school to do the very best and be the very best that they can be:

1. Analyze trends, barriers to success, or areas that need work or improvement within your organization.
2. Set up opportunities for committees to dig deeply into the problems that need to be solved and how stories captured from students, parents, teachers, school staff, school leaders, or community members can shed new light onto old problems or provide powerful insights for tackling new challenges.
3. Put forth an action plan for gaining explicit results based on the emotionally charged narratives that were examined so perceptions and attitudes can assist with initiating the reflection that will lead to solid results.
4. Provide active participants to organize shared-decision-making teams, study groups, or any other form of collective, organized learning that focuses on the ideals of collaboration based on storytelling.
5. Meet with your parent group and compile student stories that will help other students. This might feel like a gossip session, but set up some ground rules based on real topics that you feel students will benefit from. As you create boundaries, talk about confidentiality and the reason why stories might assist with putting a new idea over the top for board of education members or make a parent night incredibly helpful and pertinent when students' stories are used to guide everyone through the night.

Stories as Social Legacies

We learn unbelievable things from those who have wisdom, and stories pack *wisdom* into what you can do to help others. I've heard amazing stories from my parents and grandparents, passed down over time, and have gained more insight, more footing into understanding valuable wisdom about the history of my own life. These *social legacies* that arrive to me through stories prepare me for victory and ruin. They make me wonder about how to *be* better or *get* better. We must do the same for our classrooms and schools as much as possible and stories will help us to stay rejuvenated.

Remember, following a collective, social process for setting up opportunities for storytelling is how social efficacy brings forth new ideas. Reflection does not only exist within individualized personal or professional spaces. We can use stories to put forth a greater emphasis on shaping decision making or creating change through our own professional agency.

We all like to vent or read about each other's deepest perceptions, attitudes, or feelings because we are humans who drive emotion through storytelling. That's actually a very healthy avenue for professional growth, believe it or not. The problem is that when we tell stories (sometimes venting within our own told stories), we from time to time forget to figure out what to do next just because the stories are so powerfully charged with an array of incredible human emotion.

Johnson and Golombek (2002) capture the essence of using narratives for professional development, with such vibrant brush strokes, when discussing the importance of teachers' narratives:

> We believe that narrative inquiry conducted by teachers individually or collaboratively, tells the stories of teachers' professional development within their own professional worlds. Such inquiry is driven by the inner desire to understand that experience, to reconcile what is known with that which is hidden, to confirm and affirm and to construct and reconstruct understandings of themselves as teachers and of their own teaching.
>
> (p. 6)

It is within this spirit that moving stories to an action phase is what can construct or reconstruct our efficiencies, open up powerful learning opportunities, or spark new energies into our relationships with our students or each other – which should never be set free as just a mere emotion or feeling that then dispels itself into thin air after we read a particular story that can actually help others grow alongside us.

The beauty of capturing authentic stories is that we can respond or react to them, but then grab hold of them and utilize them for our own growth – as a means for taking action and doing *something* with them. The work of Jalongo and Isenberg (1995) put forth an initial canvas for grabbing hold of the power of educators' stories, but doing something with them to help others learn and grow, gain wisdom for professional prowess, and collaborate with others so that wisdom transfers to our colleagues even in the messiest, most unorganized ways:

> The good teacher's life is not an orderly professional pathway; rather, it is a personal journey shaped by context and choice, perspective and values. Narrative is uniquely well suited to that personal/professional odyssey. It is primarily through story, one student at a time, that teachers organize their thinking and tap into the collective, accumulated wisdom of their profession.
>
> (p. xvii)

Reflection and action are central themes within this book, and whether reflection is messy, organized, calculated, or free flowing, it is how we wrestle with ideas, gain new wisdom, and socially transmit it to others – so that we might then garner new insights and reflections as it then circles back to us within a wind-mill-recyclable fashion – is what matters for fostering opportunities for making organizational changes or solving problems.

The Top Seven Areas of Powerful Storytelling

Recognizing the seven key areas of narrative reflection that will have the most influence on your organization is essential to your success in knowing when and how to use stories that will not only set your heart on fire, but assist you to get results for your students, colleagues, and your school. Maybe you just want to use stories for initiating reflection during your new teacher orientation? Maybe you want to use stories to embark on a long-term action research project? Reflection is important, yes, but reflection without action or social consumption is useless because it will only live within a dusty vacuum.

I have received hundreds of narratives from educators all over the nation, and as I read and reflected on all of the narratives that were sent to me for this book and for future research, I noticed that there were some major similarities with how stories were being used in schools today. After

When and How to Use Authentic Stories

grouping the large pool of narratives into thematic clusters, I immediately noticed patterns and divided the narratives into the following seven topical areas that this book will focus on for helping you to improve your own craft and organizational success. Narratives that promote wonder, reflection, and the greatest change are predominantly about:

1. Relationships (school, community, and interpersonal)
2. Instruction (teaching, learning, and succeeding)
3. Assessment (formative and summative)
4. Policy construction (as a support or barrier)
5. Politics (clouding our daily tasks and abilities)
6. Motivation (strengthening both students and adults)
7. Students advocating for other students (stories written by students for other students) or helping the adults in our organization.

It is within each of these categories that powerful stories ignite the minds of educators and bring about the greatest change within an organization. While each of the following chapters in this book will deal with all seven of these categories, let's take a brief look at another story to build a framework for understanding how and when stories can be used appropriately by you or your staff. Consider this story written by an eleventh grader in Virginia:

> *I can't look at him anymore . . . not after he freaked out on Matt like that. He has a hall pass ready for Matt to go to the principal even before Matt walks into class. He is such a jerk. Sure, Matt isn't perfect, but it's like Mr. Greer just labeled him as a trouble-maker, and now when something goes wrong in class, he just assumes it's Matt's fault. If I were Matt, I'd go down to the counseling office and ask . . . no, demand . . . a different section of science even if he has to take physics, instead [of chemistry]. Mr. Greer just has it out for him and even if he doesn't or says that he doesn't, we all know what Mr. Greer thinks of Matt, anyway, just by how he acts towards him.*
>
> *– Molly Robertson, eleventh-grade student*

It is no secret that having positive teacher–student relationships creates a foundation for everything else to potentially be successful for a student – including having higher achievement results versus students who have teachers who *don't* really care or who are non-engaged learners where teachers might not respond to students as coaches, mentors, role models, or subscribers to positive reinforcement philosophies related to building up strong student motivation and support.

Notice how the narrative written by Molly focuses on the punitive aspects of a teacher's classroom management – a story which seems basic in nature because it illustrates an undesired behavior of punitive reactions to Matt – something that we might assume all teachers should know and never do. Yet, Molly reminds us how students see things from the sidelines. We learn that Molly actually feels something while reflecting on this situation, especially when Mr. Greer carries out his daily plan of getting rid of Matt. What Mr. Greer thinks works for the classroom and maintaining an order of peacefulness actually backfires when students perceive an unfair and punitive situation.

> **Wonder**: Could the story about Matt actually be used in a new teacher orientation?
> **Reflection**: In what ways can we think about the normal, daily things we do as educators and add spice to our own learning so that stories grab us by our collars and wake us up to the perceptions that students, parents, or school officials might have about any situation that is brought to their attention?
> **Change**: Write a list of people, places, and issues that you feel need to be addressed for transforming your school into a better school and then think about the stories of those you serve and how they might fit into getting others on board, coming to consensus about an issue, or proposing new initiatives that need additional funding.

There are hundreds of books written about motivating students and fostering positive relationships with students. Saenz and Dew (2015), Bentham and Hutchins (2005), and Whitaker (2003) are just a few authors who articulate the power of "It's People, Not Programs" theme within their educational leadership landmark books (Whitaker, 2003, pp. 7–12).

The question you might be asking right now is, "In what ways will reading narratives about good or bad teacher/student relationships help me to know something different about what I think I already know and believe is common sense?" Within this book, you will find narratives that illustrate some of the key factors and insights behind what students believe are the special ingredients that teachers should embody to carry out a successful classroom where students are ultimately engaged.

Students' stories can unpack deep feelings about what they feel is important for teachers to know about them and how they should behave inside and outside the classroom. From respecting a student's individuality to recognizing a powerful work ethic to knowing what motivates even the most reluctant learner, the narratives within this book that illustrate the deep connection between students and teachers will, at the very least, make you think about each and every action that you have and remind you that students are impressionable and often never forgetful. Educators can put their best foot forward and always learn something new about their students.

How to Use Stories

The *how* is very important when using narrative theory for school transformation. You don't want to bore others. You don't want stories to fall on deaf ears. You don't want to breach confidentiality. You want anonymity. You do not want embarrassment to lead your school. You have to be selective and graceful. You cannot force issues to develop by forcing stories down everyone's throat, and you don't want storytelling to lose its power because you use them too often. You don't want people to run the other way when they see you, thinking, "Oh no! Here comes Miss Oswald, that crazy social studies teacher. She constantly talks about living in Alaska when she was a kid."

Open and Honest Narratives

Drew Merchant, a middle school principal in Alabama, had monthly luncheons with his student council members. While eating sandwiches from the school cafeteria, they talked about problems that students are having with the master schedule. Drew had no idea that his students felt like "machinery in a factory of widgets" with only 20 minutes for lunch and three minutes passing time between classes.

As Drew made plans for a scheduling committee to get cracking on next year's master schedule, he invited a few students to sit in on the committee. The following story might make you laugh because it is so silly, but it was so powerful for Drew's scheduling committee to read when the students shared exactly how they felt:

> *Leslie, frazzled from a fight that she had with her mom right before school, was so upset that she needed a minute to pull herself together in the lavatory before the bell rang. The only problem was that she couldn't take more than a moment to try to compose herself. In an effort to squeeze in all of her classes into one 9-period day, the kids at Grovetown Middle barely had enough time to go to the bathroom. When lunch rolled around, 10 of the 20 minutes were lost waiting in line to get their food. Grovetown was a place where socializing was frowned upon, where recess went to die; after all, they weren't in elementary school anymore, and kids were packed into silos, drifting through their days just hoping to have one second more than the bell permitted.*
> *– Narrative read out loud to the scheduling committee by Jackie Swanson, eighth-grade student*

Jackie opened Drew's eyes. She was honest, powerful, deliberate, and focused. As a result, Drew's scheduling committee looked at what they were doing, why they were doing it, and ultimately did away with a 9th period that was set aside for "supervision" and a quasi-study hall that the kids didn't like anyway because they were tired by the end of the day.

Stories that are packed with honesty pack a punch. They open eyes. They add flavor to grandma's pot roast.

> **Wonder**: Did you miss an opportunity to really listen to your students today and take something that they were saying and apply it to your real teaching or principal life?
>
> **Reflection**: What has happened over the past few months in your school or district that you know is a problem that needs to be reviewed? Can you think of something that someone said to spark your senses

for wanting to address the issue in the first place? Can you narrativize those sentiments and share it with your review committee to add more flavor for why you need to overhaul something at your school?

Contextualized Narratives

Sarah Roberts, a twelfth-grade parent of a high school in Arkansas, coordinated the after prom party each year for the past four years. She was always happy to volunteer her time for the kids and keep them safe and sound at the school's after-party while having some fun too. When the planning committee was getting ready to put the final touches on the event last year, Sarah shared a story about a teenage pregnancy that resulted months after the prom and how the school's event should do what it can to curb teenage unprotected sex. While she shared an actual story that didn't use the student's name from previous years, the context of the story did not productively advance the planning and preparation of the after-party event.

Instead, it resulted in parents and school staff feeling disgruntled by Sarah's storytelling even though she meant well and tried to get everyone to do something about preventing any sexual conduct related to the prom. The problem with Sarah's storytelling wasn't that she wasn't honest, but that she went way above the context for the task that her committee was charged with.

Stories Shouldn't Be "Cut and Pasted"

Abbie Flynn, a fifth-grade ELA teacher in New York, received an e-mail from a parent about why her daughter was absent from school and unable to finish her project as a result. Abbie took the e-mail and cut and pasted some of the text to a Word Document and showed her students the text on her projected smartboard in order to send a message to her class about how important it is to be "responsible fifth graders who do their work each night."

Although the text could not be directly identifiable to which student was in question (because the part about "being absent" was left out), the fact that someone's e-mail was used to prove a point was not only careless, but not the type of narrative theory that this book discusses or condones.

Capturing powerful stories to cause positive change is one thing. Turning narrative theory into a series of "cuts and pastes" is something completely different than using authentic stories to ignite wonder, reflection, and change.

Getting Permission

Sometimes, it is hard to get the permission of those who tell powerful stories when they become textualized. Those who author such stories might be somewhere else. They might be our memories of a situation helping us to narrativize something that we heard from someone else. Whatever the case may be, we should strive to gather the author's permission and still use pseudonym for protecting the anonymity of those we desire to quote.

Best practice, even in the field of qualitative research, such as this, is to always, always, protect your human subjects by masking name, title, location or region, and even gender when necessary. Placing such protective protocols within your work will not only create admiration for how you value others' words and stories, but it will also protect you, legally, if what you wanted to capture really could be directly identifiable to others throughout your entire process.

Compiling Stories through Cloak and Dagger

I don't really need to say much about this one. You are not spying on others to get good stories to share with others for your organizational transformation. It sounds silly, but it still needs to be said. OK? There.

Don't Feed the Rumor Mill or Add Fillers

Using authentic stories should be just that: authentic. Not made up. Not fictitious (unless you are really good at constructing believable stories for others to think about). Your stories should be *real* and factual. They can embed tons of emotion, yes, but the stories you use to ignite others should be something that they can go back to and examine. Your stories should be relative to what educators do each day and not be something that never happened.

One of the greatest liberations of qualitative research is that it is liberal. It lets you breathe life into research. It is human and it is real. When we tell stories, we might tend to embellish what we narrativize. Sometimes, that is OK. But, most times, it becomes a nuisance for both the author and the audience. We can see true value diminish when adjectives and adverbs are filling in paragraphs. Well, people don't talk that way, at least not the educators and researchers that I've met.

So, keep it real. Keep it simple. Capture plots. Capture emotions for what they reveal. Don't force stories to unfold into Stephen King novels of mystery and suspense. Take stories for what they are: simple human experiences and emotions that never need to be over glorified. Let the stories do the work that they are intended to do.

Don't Upset the Organization

If you want to use a story, ask yourself these questions:

1. Will this story upset anyone?
2. Will this story decrease the trust that I've built within my classroom or school?
3. Will my colleagues receive something completely different from my intentions as to why I'm sharing this story in the first place?
4. Is there any risk involved with sharing this story?

Roger Farrow, a superintendent of Schools in Missouri, decided to use a narrative during a school board executive session presentation. The topic had to do with teacher negotiations and the status of any concessions that he was looking for from the bargaining unions in his district. Although the session was private and closed to the public, two of his board members took issue with some of the quotes that Roger captured from the union officials who were part of the contract committee. Roger found himself treading on thin ice when he decided to use stories to portray his failed negotiations with both the teacher union and clerical staff union.

While Roger was passionate about his work and his task for negotiating fair contracts that would both benefit the district and the unions, he used caliber rifle quotes that almost portrayed his unions as negative to his board of education members.

Capture Stories with Purpose and Passion

The title of this book uses the word "ignite." So, ignite others, please! Where there is passion, there is emotion. Where there is emotion, there is an outlet for incredible change. But, don't let that emotion become unbridled. Steer stories of power through their proper channels. Take a look at what Deidre Wilson, an assistant principal in Florida, shared with her staff at a faculty meeting presentation on creating mentor relationships with their students through a new advisory program that would help students to have teachers as quasi–big brother/big sisters after school:

> *Alisha's house was wall-to-wall roach infested. Her daddy worked the third shift and would yell at Alisha every morning when he came home from work before she went off to school. Her momma died when Alisha was four and daddy wanted the house cleaned no matter what excuses Alisha had. Alisha didn't know what to do with all of the bugs. She cried and cried and felt helpless at home. A lot for a fourth grader to shoulder. School was her happy place. There, she ate, read, and didn't have daddy's belt smacking her with all of his force when she was just trying to get ready for school each day. Alisha loved Miss Owens, her fourth-grade teacher. Miss Owens had a family of her own, but treated Alisha like another one of her daughters. Alisha stayed after school for Miss Owen's advisory club. Together, they played games, talked about science and the stars, and even talked about Alisha's dreams. Never was there a time when they talked about bugs. Alisha's world was better even if it was only because of one more extra hour added to her school day. She didn't have to think about the roaches or her daddy's fists. She even thought about what she wanted to study once she goes to college. Nine years away and big dreams and wonder crossed Alisha's landscape. All because of a teacher and an extra hour.*

Deidre didn't just ask for volunteers for the student advisory club. She tapped them on the shoulder, and they responded to her call for service to help students who were even worse off than Alisha.

You need to always think about how to capture a powerful and thoughtful focus on how to use stories in your school. In summary, here are the eight areas of *how* to effectively use stories to ignite wonder or create an "aha!" moment for your school community – even if it is planted in just one person!

- Stories need to be open and honest.
- Stories need to be contextualized.
- Stories should not be cut and pasted from regular school business correspondence.
- Stories need the originator's or author's permission *and* efforts to protect their identity.
- Stories should not be borrowed from secret faculty room cameras.
- Stories should never fuel or feed rumors within your school or district, and you never have to provide artificial ingredients to your collected stories.
- Stories should never upset your organization or jolt relationships with your trusted groups just because of your decision to use a story.
- Most importantly, stories need to be filled with purpose and passion.

Now that you have some basic guidelines for *how* to use stories in your school or district, you might be wondering *when* you could use powerful stories and what the results might be for touching hearts and spearheading reflection and change within your organization.

When to Use Stories

You can basically name the time, place, and forum for using stories in your school. They fit everywhere and can cover just about everything. Your job is to focus in on the most important areas that you want to trigger and cause change, and you can start your journey with narrativizing and sharing stories right now!

Wonder: What kinds of issues might your colleagues be working on or preparing in the following forums of *when* stories could be used, and what are the issues that need to be addressed in such forums?
- Action research groups
- Study groups
- Shared decision-making teams
- Forums for advocacy
- School board meetings
- Orientations (for students, parents, or staff)
- Parent meetings
- Conferences
- Assemblies
- Fundraising events.

"Story" Me, Don't Just Tell Me

Let me illustrate how Josh Evans, a sixth-grade teacher in Michigan, started out his "Meet the Teacher" Night before school actually started where fifth graders from the three elementary schools in his district would come to drop off their supplies, try their combination locks on their lockers, and take a tour of the school. He used this powerful narrative from one of his former sixth graders for having a powerful impact on his students and parents who attended the event:

> *I was scared out of my mind. A locker? What if I couldn't open it? What if I couldn't get my books out and then my teachers would yell at me because I was late to class or think that I was stupid. What if I get something caught in the locker like my jacket and then there would be locker grease all over my new jacket! My mom would kill me if I ruined my new jacket! She just got it for me last week – the one I really wanted too. My God, I was so scared to go to sixth grade. But, you know what? It was just a locker. It was so silly to worry about something so small like that. The locker wasn't a big deal, after all. It was the huge, hairy bully waiting for me around the corner who was gonna stuff me in*

> *the locker that I couldn't open was what I should have been worried about!*
> — Samantha Staley, now an eighth-grade student

Josh's use of Samantha's story got enormous laughter from his audience. What started out as a fear of lockers became a diminished fear of both lockers and even bullies. The incoming sixth graders laughed at the "hairy bully" depiction from Samantha's story and through Josh's use of narrative, he was able to gain allies in both his students and their parents while easing so many common fears from students who were going to now enter middle school.

Stories Can Be Powerful for All

So, what if educators tackled issues in all of the nooks and crannies of their daily lives and on all levels of leadership within their organizations? What if we relied on our own stories that speak to us about what we need to do or where we need to go within our schools that we inhabit each day as we strive to sustain powerful teaching while empowering decision making and the creative teaching craft that our students deserve?

How can narratives bring about regional approaches to solving problems or studying issues and topics? Can school board members also engage in professional learning communities where narratives are used to recruit and hire the best staff for their school district? Can student created narratives offer teachers a smorgasbord of opportunities to better know their students, what makes them tick, and how to engage them each day that they walk through your school doors?

Within each of the upcoming chapters of this book, the seven categories where stories can have the greatest impact on your program will uncover other issues that led to successful professional topics or goals, ultimately worked on within various professional learning communities, problem-solving forums, seminars, workshops, orientations, and so many other venues where social reflection can be both a personal and professional tool.

It is with this spirit that we now move to Chapter 2 to more deeply IGNITE how to use stories or narratives for improving all kinds of relationships – school, community, and interpersonal relationships. This is my favorite chapter because if we do not feed our relationships with one another, there is no one around to even care about teaching, learning, assessments, policies, or even the wildest story that your crazy grandmother might share with you.

Bibliography

Bentham, S. and R. Hutchins. (2005). *Improving student motivation together.* New York: Routledge.

Friend, M. and L. Cook. (2012). *Interactions: Collaboration skills for school professionals*, 7th edition. New York: Pearson.

Jalongo, R. and J. Isenberg. (1995). *Teachers' stories: From personal narrative to professional insight.* New York: Jossey-Bass.

Johnson, K. and P. Golombek. (2002). *Teachers' narrative inquiry as professional development.* New York: Cambridge University Press.

Karnes, F. and S. Bean. (2009). *Leadership for students: A guide for students*, 2nd edition. New York: Prufrock.

Kelley, D. (2012). *Sports fundraising: Dynamic methods for schools, universities, and youth sport organizations.* New York: Routledge.

Saenz, A. and J. Dew. (2015). *Relationships that work: Four ways to connect and set boundaries with colleagues, students, and parents.* New York: Routledge.

Sargeant, A. and E. Joy. (2014). *Fundraising management.* New York: Routledge.

Tempel, E., et al. (2010). *Achieving excellence in fundraising,* 3rd edition. New York: Rowman and Littlefield.

Whitaker, T. (2003). *What great teachers do differently: Seventeen things that matter most.* New York: Routledge.

2 | Stories that Improve and IGNITE School, Community, and Interpersonal Relationships

Everything that we do in education or anywhere else relies on the strengths of our relationships with others. Period. You can have a great lesson ready to go for your class. Your lesson won't matter if your students hate you. You can have the most disciplined students who do not "talk out of turn" (even though the best classrooms are sometimes the loudest classrooms where learning is collaborative). Your classroom management won't matter if your students hate you. You might be the best teacher in your school. But, it will be painful and lonely if your colleagues hate you. You might be loved by your principal, superintendent, or students. But, it will be painful if your students' parents don't perceive you as being their cup of tea. Get the point?

Strengthening Teacher–Student Relationships

Use Storytelling and Narrative Writing in the "Reverse"

Stories can strengthen relationships of all kinds. You can strengthen relationships with your students, colleagues, parents, and community members by sharing stories about relationships that have failed or are grave. I call this, "sharing stories in the reverse." We are prone to automatically expecting glorious stories to create bonds between one another. Sharing stories that sometimes depict the negative elements of our minds can also strengthen our relationships, especially with our students. Check out the story below which was written by Gail Sanders, a middle school teacher in

Illinois, as she used herself in a story to depict how the rules that she sets for students often also apply to her, as well:

> *Mrs. Sanders is such a hypocrite. Here we are outside for a fire drill, and I accidentally stepped on Bobby's foot while we were walking in line. Bobby let out a groan, and then we both get into trouble for talking and fooling around during a fire drill. Then, I saw Mrs. Sanders talking on her cell phone to, I don't know, maybe her husband or something. She is laughing and having a jolly old time, but we get in trouble? Why do we have to be quiet if she doesn't have to be quiet?*
> *– Suzi Reynolds, former eighth-grade student in Gail Sanders' class*

Here, Gail's students appreciated how she used herself as the subject of a narrative to illustrate a real situation that happened on a typical fire drill day a few years back when she was a new teacher. She reflected with her students that they were right: that she should have let the phone call from her own daughter wait until the fire drill was over, unless it was an emergency. Gail was able to use this narrative as an instructional tool showing that she, herself, is human, and that all humans make mistakes or can sometimes lose focus on the here-and-now.

Gail also used this narrative to teach her students how to speak up and ask questions no matter how difficult they might be. In this case, Gail taught everyone that a student from her class could have raised their hand and politely said, "Mrs. Sanders, we had to be quiet during the fire drill and you were having fun chatting with someone on your phone. Is everything OK?" Gail increased the power of her relationships with her students by inviting open, honest, and mature communication.

Don Reynolds, a high school principal in Massachusetts, used the following story with both his staff members and students to accomplish multiple topics, perspectives, and issues about smoking, rules, and fairness:

> *I get suspended for two days because I was smoking out by the South Street fence – which I guess wasn't 1,000 feet from school, yet, everyone sees Mrs. Harding go out to her car during her planning period to smoke and no one says anything to her. I told our Principal that it wasn't fair, and all he said was*

> "This is not about Mrs. Harding, Kristen. This is about you." I mean, what a joke. If there are rules for us, why don't the same rules apply to the adults who are supposed to be role models for us? Next time, I'm going to measure [laughs] 1,000 feet and draw a chalk line so when Jacobs comes running out to suspend me again, I can stand right on the line that I drew.
> – Kristen Stoddard, twelfth-grade student

Not only were relationships strengthened with Don's students during an assembly where he promised to them that he would work his hardest to not be a principal who doesn't see all sides of an issue, but his staff (except the smokers who really did sneak out to their cars for a puff) thought that the example was a great way to build a strong relationship and platform for supporting fairness for what sometimes appeared to be an unfair world in his students' lives. The last thing that Don's students respected was hypocrisy, and Don has "been there and done that before." He thought he would try using this narrative to pack a punch as he wondered what he could do to prove his points and generate learning opportunities for his young adults who often thrived on issues related to fairness and "what's good for the goose should be good for the gander" mentality.

> **Wonder**: I wonder if there are things that I do that contradict my own teaching or leading and if so, how can I use mistakes, human error, or contradictions to my advantage so that I grab hold of an opportunity to teach my students to be open and honest with me, always?
> **Reflection**: Are there some stories that I can share that will increase the capacity of my relationships with my students even if those stories are not glorious or glorified pep talks? Are there stories that I can use "in the reverse" to pack a punch and create learning opportunities?
> **Change**: I am committed to having a different kind of relationship with my students where they can learn how to effectively communicate, question, or advocate for others in a mature way that exudes self-confidence.

Reviewing Our Own Behaviors through Stories

Teachers and school leaders are humans too. We all know that. Are there things that we say and do, without even truly realizing it, that push our students away from us? Our own reflections can sometimes be our best investment into creating stronger relationships with the students we teach or the teachers we lead. Take a look at how Donna Hammish, a fifth-grade teacher in Florida, uses this generic story (not about her), but about a situation that really did take place in another teacher's classroom down the hall last year:

> *My teacher won't let me go to the lavatory any more. She says that I really don't have to go and all that I want to do is get out of having to sit in class. And she just says it out loud in front of everyone to make me look stupid. Since when does she know when I have to go to the bathroom? When I told my mom about it, she said she was going to call the school board. My mom wants to call the newspaper now and the TV stations too. [laughs] I don't care. They should be exposed. All I wanted to do was go to the bathroom. So stupid. I hate this stupid school. I should have just gotten up and went, but I was so mad. All the teachers do is power trip all day long. It's like a jail in there. I'm not a trouble-maker. They should spend their time giving the trouble-makers grief.*
>
> *– Amber Wilkins, sixth-grade student*

Donna used this narrative to confront the idea of students trying to get away from doing their work by pretending to go to the lavatory (or needing to go to the lavatory). In reality, Amber really needed to use the lavatory, and all of her previous "the boy who cried wolf" attempts caught up with her when she really needed to excuse herself from the lesson.

Donna's creativity in using this narrative demonstrated to her students that she would try her hardest to make learning powerful, but there would be times that her students wouldn't always love what they were doing and they still would need to get the task completed.

As a result, Donna came up with a card system which helped students to realize when they've tuned out and when they were struggling to stay on task by using an incredibly high level of self-awareness and emotional metacognition to help them determine when they needed an "out box" break. This narrative worked its magic on so many levels and, ultimately, the relationships that Donna had with her class increased the capacity for learning, teaching, and gaining respect because she cared about her students every single minute of the day.

Promoting Educators Who Care

Our students have real feelings and emotions about us *and* about their peers and parents. We cannot forget that for every action or reaction, there is either a victory or a consequence in the making. Take a look at some of the stories about student identity, caring, and how teachers can connect with our students to foster even greater relationships. The following students reside in Arizona and offered to share their stories for this book:

> *I hate school. My teachers don't really understand me, either. Just because I have a shaved head and like skateboards, I get looked at "funny." Who are they to judge? So, I'm not wearing a dress like their stereotypical vision of what a girl is supposed to look like. That's their problem. So, I don't write about unicorns, castles, and everything that's nice and I can't stand Taylor Swift, either. I like to write about vampires and magical aliens, instead. I like to listen to Drake and Rage Against the Machine. Thank God I have a journal where I can write about everything that I love even if everyone else hates it.*
>
>   – Casey Williams, eleventh-grade student

> *I'm so lucky to have Mrs. Stevens. No one else cares about me. My other teachers hassle me about being late, not turning in any of my homework, or sleeping in class. They have no clue that my mom is a drunk and is hardly ever home. Mrs. Stevens talks to me. She took me to McDonald's a couple of times, even. She helped me with my homework to pass her class. Everyone else could care less. All they say to me is, "You aren't going to get into college if you keep this up," or "You're going to repeat the grade and your friends are going to move ahead and leave you behind if you refuse to do your work." Little do they know that I take care of my seven-year-old sister all the time. I help her with her*

> *homework, cook, clean, and get her ready for school. By that time, I just collapse on the couch and am lucky just to even wake up in the morning and make it here [to school] on my own.*
>
> – Jessie Carter, tenth-grade student

Both of these stories tug at our hearts and both of these stories tell us something about our students' feelings, their lives, and what they go through each day. We learn about their talents, desires, dislikes, hardships, and so much more. Narratives can drive us through a roller coaster of varying degrees and even when emotions run high, our relationships with our students can strengthen even if the fuel of the narrative is powerfully diesel.

> **Wonder**: I wonder what my students are thinking right now. How can I create an environment where my relationship with them is my #1 priority?
>
> **Reflection**: Where might I use these types of stories in my school or classroom? Can I think of any situations or contexts where these stories will pack the biggest punch for causing me to change my already terrific relationships with students into even more powerful relationships? Can I think of a few stories from my own experience as a teacher or school leader that could be narrativized and then used to show my students that I care about them, that I never want to harm them, that I want to engage them and make learning meaningful, and that I will never judge or mock them?

Stories that Promote Learning and Expertise

The stories that we use to increase our relationship capacity with our students don't always have to be emotion-laden. We can select stories that will get to the heart of issues that focus on instruction and expertise. Take a look at this story which offers wisdom about the role and power of posting student work in order to showcase model work for all learners:

> *If I place student projects in the hallways, kids just come by and trash them. I don't have eyes in the back of my head, you know. When I put up a good paper – a good essay or*

> *a high grade with stars on it, the kid who wrote the paper gets teased at lunch and called the "teacher's pet" and stuff like that. It doesn't matter if I put something up in the hall or not. It seems like it causes more trouble than not doing it at all. Plus, I guess it only matters what the student and his or her parents think, but when Mr. Jenkins comes by and tells me that my bulletin boards out front are bare, he gets upset with me. I try to tell him that everything gets trashed, but he thinks that I'm just being lazy. It's a no-win situation, I guess. Respecting each other's work is a goal down the road, maybe. I know Mr. Jenkins has lots of more pressing issues right now.*
>
> *– Stephanie Claremont, fifth-grade teacher*

Using this story "in reverse," Stephanie was able to illustrate to her students how respecting each other's work is part of learning and growing. While teacher–student relationships are extremely important, also focusing on the quality of student–student relationships (especially within this scenario) can have an impact on raising student achievement and contributing to an effective school culture for all. And, we are not just talking about fostering positive student civility where bullying or vandalism is addressed within the school culture. Valuing student work leads to increased student achievement. When sample work or student exemplars that reach a high standard can be replicated, student learning and achievement also certainly increase.

While Stephanie might be frustrated with how other students do not appreciate high-quality work even in the fifth grade, Mr. Jenkins actually has a golden opportunity to work with the entire school on promoting student–student relationships through the lens of valuing school work, creating a culturally driven high powered work ethic, and growing from others' learning, while achievements can also be celebrated by both students and staff, collectively.

Here are two more stories about the power of engagement, expertise, technology usage, and teaching like a fun maniac (which students *love*)!

> *Everyone loves Mr. Reynolds. Everyone. He is hilarious. He has a wall behind his desk which has so many cool things on it . . . his track trophies from high school, his college degrees,*

Stories that IGNITE Relationships

framed, you know, stuff like that. And when he teaches, oh my God, watch out. It's like getting a ticket to a rock concert and comedy show every day. This guy is hilarious. I've never learned history through puppet shows and mixing beats. The first day, he tore a social studies book like Robin Williams in Dead Poets' Society. [laughs] I love going to school. I wish all of my teachers were like him, especially Mr. Yemmer. It's like he is jealous of Reynolds or something. He's always like, [mimicking] "You can have fun on your own time. You have to know this material by remembering it and the more fun you have, the less time you have for more content. My students always leave my class knowing more." Reynolds has like a black belt in teaching or something. He's the real sensei.

– Jordan Murphy, ninth-grade student

Ms. Beecher is like, so cool. We can tweet with her and I'm Facebook friends with her too. She always gets back to us if we leave a message for her. Ms. Beecher is so awesome. She posts funny pictures and has us figure out captions for them. Some of my friends come up with silly, over-the-edge racy captions, but Ms. Beecher doesn't seem to care. She wants us to be creative. It's like doing homework, but fun homework.

– Josh Briner, twelfth-grade student

Reflection: Are there stories that I could share that will be directly related to growing a value for student learning and achievement?

Strengthening Staff–Staff Relationships

Up to this point, we have focused on strengthening educator–student relationships even though many of the stories described above can be used for strengthening the relationships with multiple groups. Would you agree that life can be very painful if you are ostracized by your colleagues or left alone in a silo of your own teaching world? Are there instances where you have not gotten along with a staff member or viewed them as inferior or poor teachers or school leaders? Do we sometimes feel like our content area is more important than other content or subject areas in our school? I think we all have felt so many of these common, natural human feelings. We are passionate about what we do as educators and leaders. We sometimes get so into things that we can easily forget how the entire system needs to work together, collaboratively for overall success to thrive. We also don't want anyone to "see us sweat."

Notice how John Newcomb, an assistant principal in Rhode Island, used the following narrative to make a connection to his staff by reminding them that everything we do for children is important, and no one's area or expertise is better than the person down the hallway from us:

> *Oooh . . . we saw Mr. Kelly and Mr. Flanagan going at it in the hallway. Mr. Kelley was tellin' Mr. Flanagan how his class is just as important as Mr. Flanagan's, and all Mr. Flanagan kept sayin' was, "Your kids don't have to do well on a State Assessment at the end of the year, so whose class is more important now?" We thought they were going to get into a fist fight. Mr. Flanagan kept raising his coffee cup at Mr. Kelly. We were dying laughing. Here, we are told to not behave like that and they get to yell at each other in the hall?*
>
> *– Alisha Roberts, eighth-grade student*

As professional relationships with one another are sometimes defined by whom we like and whom we don't like, there is something to be said about all of the adult issues that we have to work through on our end with our colleagues – issues that shouldn't place students in the middle. At the end of the day, we know what's right and we know that teaching and leading can be exhausting. Sometimes we show our teeth, but we really don't mean to. Education is an emotional arena and teachers are passionate about their craft, their profession, and want to truly maximize their instruction time since the school year dwindles away so quickly when holidays, snow days, assemblies, and other factors impact the total amount of instruction time within a typical school year.

What is most interesting about this narrative is that Mr. Kelly and Mr. Flanagan were experiencing some frustration with the master schedule at their school regarding when music lessons were scheduled. This narrative was actually used by the teacher union to spark further discussions at

Washington Middle School about maximizing orchestra, band, and music lesson time during the day, rather than outside of school hours (before and after school practice was typical at Washington Middle School).

Hundreds of books have been written on the importance of fostering powerful collaborations, professional learning communities, and subgroup committee alliances for "solving organizational problems and increasing collaborative teacher capacity" within educational organizations. It is no epiphany that as teachers work closely together, effective organizational decisions increase, whereby positively effecting student learning and student programming. What appeared to be a potential "fight" between Mr. Kelly and Mr. Flanagan was actually used to spark deep conversations about structural problems that these two teachers were having.

Don't Forget Coaches and Anyone Else in Your Organization

Coaches are important too. They have an incredible power with and sometimes over our student athletes who often live to play and play to live. Notice how Richard Collins, a superintendent in North Carolina, used this narrative with his students during a parent–athlete information night for Fall sports signups:

> *Coach Falmer benches us if our grades are not above a C in any class. It doesn't matter if it's tech. class, science, or phys. ed. He has a Twitter account just with the Grandville High teachers so they can post a message to him right up to the last minute before practice or a game. If we don't pull our grades up, we're off the team. Falmer doesn't play. He's all about making us better men. Responsible. Hard working. I respect him even if he's tough. He reamed me out one time because I blew off my social studies research project. Even though I'm his starting quarterback, I was benched. My dad was mad at Falmer, but Falmer didn't back down. He doesn't care who we are. First string or third. Colleges looking at us or not. That dude is hard core. I guess he's lookin' out for us.*
> *– Tyrell Sanford, twelfth-grade student*

Creative uses of narratives, on all levels of the organization, is a way to strengthen relationships with students (and even parents in this scenario) versus having Richard, as superintendent simply stand on stage and say that "coaches will be monitoring student academics." Instead, he packed a punch and hit a home run with creating an atmosphere of humanness to his presentation.

Be Careful with Your Staff

In Chapter 1, we discussed some of the instances where judgment is needed to contextually share stories so you do not send an earthquake within your organization. When you are in a school, sitting next to your colleagues, stories become harder to share especially in reverse, so be careful by not getting too carried away with trying to prove a point or make a connection that actually unplugs your staff from you. In so many instances, I have seen educators attempt to share a story with good intentions, but it blows up in their faces. Take a look at how Dexter Wallace, a principal in Mississippi, used the following story, but actually ostracized Miss Rogers, a particular teacher, even when the name and grade were protected by pseudonym:

> It's almost as if my students didn't learn anything last year. Every single time I go over a fifth-grade concept that they should have learned, the students tell me that Mr. Edwards never taught them that. I don't know what to think about his abilities as a teacher. This is the second year in a row that my students didn't learn the foundational knowledge that they need to be able to do sixth-grade material. Especially in math. You have to grow math concepts, cumulatively. You can't just start teaching algebra when students don't even understand basic number canceling techniques on both sides of an equation with "x's" and "y's." I've basically had it with doing Mr. Edwards' work and then it reflects on me if the kids don't do well.
>
> – Miss Rogers, fifth-grade teacher

Although the topic of creating a consistent instructional program, where students' virtual pathways enable them to learn the same content so that they were not unprepared for the next grade-level content, is a powerful idea to flesh out, using a story, like this, in reverse, under the conditions of being a smaller school with very few grade-level teachers turned Dexter's staff members into ignoring their own wonder about the issue at hand to a negative wondering of trying to figure out who Miss Rogers really was.

Strengthening Educator–Parent and Community Relationships

You can gain allies with your community and parents by using stories that tug at their hearts, build up students in a positive manner, or also to flesh out humanistic ways to solve real problems in schools even if you think the problem is small. Sometimes, the small problems are the ones, when solved, that can go a long way in helping to build up support, trust, or motivation for someone to do something or take action on finding a solution to a nagging problem.

Gretchen Worthington, a superintendent in New York, used the following story when presenting a recommendation to her board of education to increase the length of the school year and decrease the number of half days that only pressed her parents to find child care or stay home from work when students were not in school:

> *Count up all the days that my child is actually learning in school. Take the 180 days for the mapped out school year, minus three snow days, minus five early release days so teachers can do professional development, minus Fridays before holiday vacations where it is a blow-off and my daughter tells me that she just watches movies, minus 10 days taking assessments throughout the year, and what is she left with? Less than 160 days of instruction out of a 365-day year? That is just ridiculous! What are we doing? God. No wonder other countries are outperforming us!*
> *– Mary Reidenfield, fourth- and eleventh-grade parent*

Using a real story from a real parent, versus simply reporting to the school board that more instructional time was needed, immediately peaked interest and support for Gretchen's recommendation to be approved, unanimously, by the school board. Sure, there were other factors and data that were used to make her points powerful, but this story did one amazing thing: it raised eyebrows.

Gretchen also used the following story when unveiling a new cafeteria menu for her entire school district and the narrative was taken from her own Director of Operations who oversaw the Food Service Dept. within the district:

> *It's become like a joke now. The kids call the hotdogs "green." The lunch ladies say that they are turkey hotdogs. They do have a greenish hue under the warming trays, though [laughs]. Who wants a turkey hot dog anyway? Why can't the kids have real hotdogs? Most of the students are bringing their lunches now, anyway, because there isn't anything that they want besides salad, which looks normal, but how much salad can a kid eat? And, teachers tell the kids that they are supposed to be eating healthier so that's why they have this kind of food? Hotdogs that look alien? Can't food be healthy and taste good too?*
>
> *– Edward Walters, Director of Operations*

While "green" hotdogs seem like a problem that is far down on the priority list of more important problems, the food menu did need an overhaul, and the students actually cheered when they found out that there would no longer be turkey hotdogs being served in their schools.

This "hot dog story," among the other stories presented within this chapter, created strong bonds between educators and their students, among colleagues, parents, and even school board members and they exuded emotion, truth, openness, and bluntness, as well.

> **Wonder**: Are there small problems that need to be solved? Is there something that has been outstanding for a long time that needs elbow grease? Is there something that is nagging on your classroom, school, or district?
>
> **Reflection**: Can you identify at least three problems or issues, even if you think they are tiny problems, which will directly help students?
>
> **Change**: I will create strong relationships and get ready to IGNITE teaching and learning by turning the page to Chapter 3.

Stories that IGNITE Powerful Instruction with Reduced Variance

The concept of this chapter is simple: when there is huge variance across teaching practices – which may not be considered "best" teaching practices, instructional delivery, pedagogy, policy enforcement, assessment tools used within an organization, etc., the greater the variance will be for overall school-wide success and increased student achievement.

Certainly, this book does not contend that teachers should be cast from the same mold, made to be robotic, or use the same mundane basal reader while teaching from the same exact page, as some of their colleagues might do each day. Instead, it is appropriate to assume that there are "best" teaching practices and then there are "poor" teaching practices, conversely. It is the variance of the "best" living with the "poor" that must be eradicated in order for a school to improve, systematically, not just marginally.

Some common areas of variance occur within the topics of technology, grading, and even student recess time. This chapter will continue to include real narratives from real educators, students, and parents so we could elaborate more on the discussion of how stories can help educators to tackle instructionally related topical areas.

Although relationships fare to be the most important factor contributing to student success, we cannot ignore that teaching and learning is why students go to school in the first place. Take a look at how Sophia's story below leads us right into the importance of how instruction can easily become varied from teacher to teacher:

Instruction

> We never know anything about what is going to be on a social studies test. Mrs. Longfellow just tells us to study. Then, we go to our next class and learn that we are having another test tomorrow – this time in science. When we think we've hit rock bottom, we find out that Mr. Gillen is giving us a math quiz on the same day. That's three tests all in the same day! What are they trying to kill us or something? You know by the time I get back from my swim meet and my dad picks me up, it's going to be like 8:00. Then, I try to eat super quickly so I can study until falling asleep at my desk at 11:00 or 12:00. They tell us to be well rounded, but I'm just exhausted. And, I'm just a kid still!
> – Sophia Bauer, ninth-grade student

When Mrs. Longfellow handed out exit tickets to her students one day and invited them to provide any feedback that would help them do better in her class, Sophia shared her story with her.

What resulted from Sophia's narrative was an effort led by Mrs. Longfellow to speak at a Twin Hills High School Faculty Meeting where the topic had to do with staff communication about scheduling quizzes, tests, or assessments and the urgency for teachers to use exit tickets in their classes. "Sometimes, students don't feel comfortable talking to a teacher, but they might share something with us in writing," said Mrs. Longfellow.

> What resulted from our faculty meeting was a more concerted effort to gauge student feedback and also use our e-mail calendar to publicly display when we were all giving tests in the ninth-grade sections of ELA, social studies, science, and math – the core subjects – so students could learn better by being prepared and not falling asleep at home when studying.

Best practices for creating high-quality learning, teaching, and assessments do exist and there have been hundreds of books written about using solid, research-based, best practices in the areas of differentiation, coteaching, classroom management, literacy, grading, and so much more. Landmark books, such as those written by *Beninghof (2012)*, *Brookhart (2014)*, *Cerri (2012)*, *Curran (2015)*, Dueck (2014), and *Marzano (2003)* are just to name a few authors that touch upon various arenas of educational learning, instruction, and assessment.

In the above narrative example, exit tickets and avoiding schedule-crowding were two major ways in which Mrs. Longfellow was able to help her students with specific learning and assessment task outcomes. Sophia's grades improved when she wasn't studying for three tests on one particular day, and her classmates capitalized on providing their teachers with powerful feedback for making their school experiences *better* school experiences.

> **Wonder**: Do you wonder if there is anything that you do, inadvertently, that is not always a best practice? Do you wonder if students will learn better and learn more if there were safeguards set up in your program to ensure that you are always doing the best, as a school or district, not just a classroom, so that everyone can benefit from a powerful education?
> **Reflection**: What can you do starting tomorrow that will be a best practice that you could share with other teachers or school leaders?
> **Change**: You can be a change agent by building up a consistent program that becomes a thoughtful program on all levels of addressing students' real concerns.

Digital Blindness

There is an ongoing discourse and debate about the necessity of having digital classrooms versus using traditional methods. There is a search for the best methods and for balance. The use of print materials is important, perhaps, or a blended learning approach is something that might also be an option. Schools must figure out where the balance will come from.

According to a recent survey conducted by Common Sense Media (2015), "tween and teen screen time has increased to approximately six to nine hours of daily usage time which includes modes consisting of television, video streaming, video or mobile gaming, social media, and so much more." As a result, schools strive to figure out how to engage learners, while keeping modern trends afloat by permitting digital knowledge consumption tools in the classroom (i.e. tablets, smartphones, laptops, netbooks, etc.). Embedded within the school curriculum and resource tool shed, students are now taking more online assessments, schools are purchasing more e-books, and school leaders are also looking for digital ways to lead their school organizations, according to Anderson (2014).

Navigating through the digital business of schooling and potentially providing students with digital tools for learning was an interest of the Cayuga City School District in Vermont. Before district leaders made any decisions on the role that technology would play in their schools, students in grades 6–12 were given a survey to determine what students thought about the multiple uses of technology in their classrooms. This student survey was used as part of the decision making for their school district to consider moving to an all-digital platform for textbooks, a 1:1 Chromebook initiative, and cloud-based student management programs.

The results of the student survey were very interesting. Over 55% of students did not want to move towards a digital school and 30% of the remaining 45% of students articulated the desire to keep reading print materials – especially paperback trade books for both fiction and nonfiction selections.

As a result of this survey, the brakes were hit on adopting an incredibly expensive initiative that school officials thought was going to be a "slam dunk" for stakeholders who were lobbying for digital solutions for Cayuga. Cayuga staff members also chimed in by providing their own perceptions and feedback regarding what everyone thought was going to be a modern, inevitable solution for moving Cayuga forward into the modern world. Take a look at what Rhonda Arlington shared with Cayuga staff members during a faculty meeting which focused on blended learning strategies:

> Why does everything have to be digital? Digital textbooks, digital homework, videos, iPads, Chromebooks. . . . What happened to good old pens, paper, and books? Half the time, I have to tend to technical issues in the classroom. The kids forget their passwords. The Wi-Fi isn't working. There is only 20% battery life left and not enough plugs for the kids. Typing a word document on a tablet or small netbook is such a pain in the butt. The kids actually hate it. They'd rather sit at a

> *desktop computer with a normal-sized keyboard to do their work. Often, the devices need updates loaded into them, as well. I wonder how much instructional time is lost just by fixing up all of these procedural things.*
>
> *– Rhonda Arlington, tenth-grade ELA teacher*

While the majority of Cayuga students felt that relying on digital solutions for instruction was not very attractive to them because "they spend so much time on their own devices at home that they need some sort of break from looking at display screens when they get to school," as one eleventh-grade student commented, Rhonda articulated some practical reasons to not lobby for additional technology within the curriculum even though we all know that classrooms across America need technology if student survival in the workforce is going to take place.

However, through the use of student perception narratives – which were compiled with the survey results and staff members' narratives, such as the one written by Rhonda, another local school district faced similar inquiries about technology when a new superintendent was hired. He decided to move forward with an all-inclusive digital platform for the Twin Pines School District.

As a result, stakeholders within the Twin Pines community used various narratives, both supporting and refuting technology, to spark discussion for creating a subcommittee within the district that researched and analyzed balanced solutions for entering into the digital world. What the superintendent didn't want, however, was increased variance – where some classrooms used technology and others didn't.

This was not necessarily an opposition to technology; it was more or less an opposition to using technology that worked, having an infrastructure set up that could support student users, and not becoming frustrated by the ailments of failed technology.

Take a look at another narrative that prompted research teams at Cayuga to research more about the effects of technology on student achievement:

> *How powerful is technology? I . . . I think what I mean is . . . do we have any proof that technology raises student achievement in Cayuga? Do we know, for sure, that if we move to a 1:1 initiative that we are making a decision that shows us that it really works? I'm not for or against technology, so you*

> *won't find me being pushy about it either way, but what I do want to know is how are we going to measure it? How are we going to prove it? And, if the kids told us that they still like using books, how are we going to balance everything at our schools? Just sayin' . . . we really need to have a plan to share with the taxpayers when we present anything to the community or ask for money through a capital project. You know, stuff like that.*
>
> *– Ginger Peterson, twelfth-grade business teacher*

What was learned by both Cayuga and Twin Pines was that using perception data through the form of narratives was helpful for launching a research committee that could look carefully at the pros and cons of delivering a digital campus in 2017–2018. Such eye-opening narratives posed opportunities for deep reflection among teachers, parents, technology specialists, the superintendent of schools, and board of education members. Ginger Peterson supplemented the discussion by urging the technology research committee to come up with specific goals and tracking methods to use for measuring the impact of technology in the classroom as it relates to increasing student achievement. The initiative wanted to invite the reduction of variance in the instructional program. There shouldn't be "haves" (those who have devices) and "have nots" (those who don't) in their school district.

In the case of Rhonda's narrative, other districts were able to troubleshoot potential issues, save money, and decrease variance so that technology was not used only in small pockets around the school district. Instead, decisions at Twin Pines were made to purchase all-in-one desktop computers for each classroom within the district where students would be responsible for working in small collaborative groups on research, presentations, and project-based learning requirements. While desktop computers almost seem archaic to the vast market that is full of wireless devices, the desktop computers were faster, more robust, needed little to no technical service, and stored more hard drive data even though we all use clouds to store information.

Students still were also able to use and read "fresh, new, crisp novels with flashy covers that they could hold in their hands without adjusting a brightness button to cut down on their eye strain," according to Gino Grizante, Cayuga Student Council President. A balanced school district which emphasized blended learning became the focus, not an initiative where technology took over and replaced everything else that was still motivational for students.

While this is just one example of a few school districts, it is important to note that each school or district will have unique stories about their experiences and move in directions that are governed by their leadership and shared decision-making teams. While the decision to not move forward with a 1:1 digital initiative across the district was what Cayuga and Twin Pines ultimately decided, other districts might decide to do just the opposite based on their own contexts, cultures, action research or pilot studies outcomes, and governance. Either way, a program that minimizes variance should be built.

Stories that urge reflection on a particular matter, through a particular lens, and through a context and culture which is often unknown at the start of any healthy debate is what is important to know about narrative-based reflection. The decision of Twin Pines to pull back on an extensive 1:1 initiative was narrative-based, yes, but culturally defined as perceptions helped the research committee to know where it has been, where it might want to go, but where it will ultimately end up as a result of powerful conversations and deep reflection through whatever story or series of stories were presented for "food for thought."

The remarkable part of all of this is that both Cayuga and Twin Pines are continuing their action research through project-based student learning objectives to determine the impact and results that technology has in the classroom environment. That, in itself, is a victory for students.

> **Wonder**: Do you need to tweak the way that you collect information so that a reduction in program variance is also a goal?
> **Reflection**: What are some inconsistencies in your instructional program that you can think of, and how might you learn how to make a powerful shift into doing something differently so that variance is reduced?
> **Change**: You can examine any aspect of your program and see how it matches up to your school or district, at large.

Teaching "Responsibility"

As we looked at some issues about technology using specific stories and responses, new knowledge was constructed and new research began for working through ideas of technology integration for both Cayuga and Twin Pines. Reflections through stories or narratives can also help educators to not only gain new knowledge, but strip down old belief systems in order to build new ones. The results of such deep reflection and self-analysis can be incredible for students, teachers, and school leaders.

What if a teacher who had a homework policy for many years was confronted by students who felt that such a policy was unfair? Is this a form of treason? Should students be a part of policy construction? Should an adult's expertise ever be questioned? Wouldn't we be offended if a student felt that we were being punitive? Or, would we embrace the difference of opinion, reflect on what we see and hear about our own behaviors, actions, policies, methods of instruction, or anything else that we do which concerns students? Should we step back and re-evaluate what we do? Should we re-evaluate with others, collectively, as well?

Let's take a look at a long-standing issue in education that many teachers and school leaders have dealt with and see how some identity reconstruction took place in the Mapleview Consolidated School District. A middle school student, Rachel Topolski, provided a copy of a homework policy from her science teacher, Mr. Wilkins, which is outlined below:

> *If an assignment is not completed by its due date, the student will receive a 0%. The student must make up the assignment after school or the additional penalty will be a 10% reduction on the next assignment even if it is turned in completed. If the student makes the assignment up after school, the 0% will not change, but the additional penalty of 10% off of a completed next assignment will not be issued.*

Here is Rachel's response to Mr. Wilkins' homework policy:

> *I'm bound to fail. All we get is penalty after penalty, and even if we make something up, we still don't get any credit? In Mrs. Overfield's class, if we miss an assignment and make it up, she gives us an 80%. So, what is the reason for Wilkins' policy? All it does is make me not want to do any work to see if he'll keep deducting 10%, then 20%, then 30% until I'm so far in the hole that I come out with a negative grade in his class? It would be funny because how do you put a negative*

> grade on a report card? This is so stupid. I even tried talking to Wilkins one day after class and all he said was, "It is my job to teach you responsibility." I wanted to tell him, "No, it's a teacher's job to help me learn, not be here to just give red zeros at the top of my five-week grade report." He has no idea about what I'm going through. My dad lost his job and my mom wants a divorce. It's chaos at my house. Some nights I just cry myself to sleep. Then, I gotta worry about not getting any credit even when I stay after school – which is better for me to do my homework, anyway, since I hate being home.
>
> – Rachael Topolski, eighth-grade student

Mr. Wilkins heard about Rachel's concerns from her counselor, Mrs. Wheatley. Interested in the conundrum and advocating for Rachel, Mrs. Wheatley approached Mr. Wilkins in school the next day during one of his planning periods. She sat down and had a one to one conversation with Mr. Wilkins and posed all sorts of scenarios for looking at his homework policy and rethinking how he might adjust it to not only help Rachel, but all students both currently and in the future. Mr. Wilkins was upset about not wanting Rachel to think that "she won" if he was going to change his policy.

Mr. Wilkins understood the competing perception about his homework policy; yet, he wasn't fully convinced that he should do anything differently. Mr. Wilkins felt very strongly about the importance of teaching Rachel "responsibility," and he responded to Mrs. Wheatley's advocacy for Rachel with hypothetical business-world scenarios, such as, "When Rachel gets a job, she isn't going to be allowed to come in a little late all the time or hand in her work to her supervisor when she wants to hand it in." Mrs. Wheatley looked at Mr. Wilkins, whom she always had a good working relationship with, and said,

> Bill . . . just to let you know . . . when we asked teachers to sign their classes up in the main office for the field day activities, you missed the deadline and now your class isn't scheduled. Should I punish the kids because you forgot or didn't do it? Should I teach you responsibility by leaving your class off the final schedule? No. I signed you up myself when I reviewed the scheduling sheet.

Mr. Wilkins just grinned, as reported by Mrs. Wheatley.

What is most interesting about Rachel's narrative is that Mrs. Wheatley removed Mr. Wilkins' name off of the homework policy, removed Rachel's name off of the narrative story, and used the tools as a discussion topic for one of her local district-wide counselor's meetings. That was a safe place, a safe forum, and it didn't hurt the organization. It was a contextually thoughtful place to have a discussion with colleagues who were like-minded professionals. The discussion had to do with the power of using explicit communication strategies to help advocate for students no matter what the issues were.

As a result of this counselor's meeting, various principals in the Mapleview District facilitated school-wide faculty meetings, at the request of the superintendent, in order to have open discussions about classroom policies, grading, homework, and so much more. Rachel's narrative sparked adult collaboration through focus groups for staff development where research was reviewed in the areas of homework, grading, and policy construction. Mapleview school leaders also held a study group where the work of Marzano (2007) and (2009) and Dueck (2014) were read and analyzed by the staff for arriving at new ways to think about their own grading policies.

Mapleview Superintendent, Gene Morrow, summed up his plans, for deeper study within these topical areas of learning and instruction, best:

> *We can't have one classroom with one late homework policy and another one across the hall with a different policy where students then just pit teachers against teachers or students label teachers as "unfair" and then parents will then call to request a certain teacher because the other one has a policy that doesn't make any sense. Rachel is right. Responsibility is important, but not at the mercy of helping kids learn. Plus, Rachel had so much going on in her life. She is just a kid and we need to give her some slack. She's a good kid and gets everything done, just sometimes not on time like the rest of us.*

Variance at Mapleview was reduced because Rachel decided to speak up and the professionals within the district decided to reflect, reshape identities that were, perhaps, situated over time and learn more, together. These stories packed punches and move a system to change.

Wonder: Do you wonder if there is anything that you do each day which might seem unfair to students? Do you ever dig your heels into the ground and stand firm on an issue that might not be so firm, after all?

Reflection: Can you think of two things that you can question about your own practices as an educator of school leader and then think about a way to reduce variance by collaborating with your school or department to see if there is something that is being done differently than how you are doing it?

Change: You can advocate for students even if going up against other adults is your only means.

The Power of Feedback

So, what happens to those assignments that students hand in and never see again for a number of weeks? Sure, teachers are extremely busy and bogged down with more paperwork than ever, but do we know just how our students feel when they do not receive something back from their teachers? Many students might not care, but through the stories shared with me from hundreds of educators across the nation, most students actually *do care* about receiving feedback from their teachers in a timely fashion. Maybe students just need to hear back from their teachers, and maybe teachers need to hear how important feedback is to their students.

Narratives, then, can spark communication between students and educators, have them reflect on their practices, and then forge ahead with quick and easy ways for students to receive feedback in all of their classes so little to no variance exists, collectively, as a school-wide initiative.

The logic here is simple: teachers who provide immediate feedback help students to achieve at higher levels than those who do not provide timely feedback. Take a look at what Randi, a student in West Virginia, has to say about one of her classes:

> *Mr. Russel gives us a test and then we don't see it for like two weeks. We turn in our journals and we don't see those either. Maybe a month later. I know he has to read all of this stuff, but c'mon. . . . I have to do my homework. Why can't he do his? Then, I get my report card and it says 80% for the quarter.*

> *How did I get an 80%? I thought I was, at least, in the 90s. It is so frustrating. Then, my mom gets mad at me because she thinks I've been blowing off the semester. If I knew I screwed something up, I could have gone in after school.*
> – Randi Owens, tenth-grade student

In a world where many schools and school districts use student management or task systems, such as Infinite Campus, Class Dojo, or E-School, where teachers post daily assignments, provide weekly updates, and help students to recognize what assignments they are missing, the issue of providing effective feedback is only partially solved with such digital solutions. Sometimes, there is not enough information for a student to know how to proceed. Sometimes, we enter grades into our systems, digitally, but there is little to no room for providing powerful feedback. Educators are busy. I know that. Trust me, I do understand. But, at what costs will student achievement suffer because we focus on some of the things that suck away our time and forget to follow through on what is important?

While all of this is a step in the right direction for getting students to become owners of their own learning progress, it is the element of providing specific, standards-based feedback that assists students to achieve at higher learning rates, according to Askew (2000), Brookheart (2008), and Pollack (2011). At Lansburg High School where Randi attends, administrators and teacher union representatives met over a six-week period during after-school planning team meetings to problem solve ways in which more effective feedback could be communicated to students across all grade levels.

While the school uses grade-level teacher–mentors for fostering the sustainment of positive relationships among students and faculty, Lansburg decided to facilitate a feedback program across the entire school where Fridays were used for student progress meetings at the end of the day. Student management systems provided a new field for teachers to insert foot notes more easily, and when students needed to know something right away about a project or assignment, they would receive a text alert that pointed them to the system's feedback field. Now that's technology!

Students loved this new program because they would walk away from handing in an assignment to knowing when to stay after school for additional help or what was still outstanding with the work that they already handed in to their teachers. Some examples of feedback texts alerts looked like this:

> *"Hi Jennifer: Your works cited list on assignment #18 needs at least four more citations before you receive a final grade for your paper on Milton."*

> *"Roger: Stop by after school so you can re-glaze your ceramic vase. It still looks faded and I wanted you to know before I put the final batch in the kiln."*

> *"Chloe: Check out your grades on the last two chapter reviews from your critical viewpoints assignments. I'll let you re-do them for a better grade since I found that your themes on both of them did not align to the proper texts that you used."*

As teachers work hard to provide feedback, grade student work, and keep up with the demands of creating daily lesson plans for various class sections, sometimes feedback is inadvertently forgotten. Yet, students want to know where they stand and seeing a grade on an assignment does not tell students much about what they need to do, how they need to do it, or when they can fix their work to make it correct or better.

Certainly, teachers can just tell students what they need to know when they see them in class, but this is not always the reality in schools. Students and teachers are sometimes absent. Students often do not attend a class section each day, but perhaps every other day. Sometimes, work needs to be done in a more timely manner than just waiting until the following week. Sometimes, we just forget because we are all human.

Whatever the case might be, digital solutions for providing feedback was what worked for Lansburg, and it all came about from a few narratives that sparked professional reflection so educators of Lansburg could arrive at the best solution for their students.

> **Wonder**: Do you ever wonder about ways that you could make your students' lives easier? Do you ever think about how technological management tools can be used creatively to reduce variance?

Reflection: Think of your own feedback system that is in place for students. What can you do differently starting tomorrow that will provide instant feedback that is quality feedback?
Change: Students want your feedback to be timely. They might not tell you that, but they do.

The Redundant Curriculum

Does your school have any data that prove that doing the same thing over and over each year increases student learning, student engagement, or student achievement? What might your students say about doing something that their older brother, sister, or parent did with the same teacher in the same classroom at the same grade level? In this case, project-based learning is not a bad thing, nor are longhouse projects when studying Native Americans. Veteran teachers aren't "bad," either. The problem here is when variance exists due to methods of teaching that are never revised – especially when surrounding colleagues are moving towards more modern methods of instruction using more innovative techniques. Take a look at Amber's narrative and the discussion that follows. It is funny, yes, but so powerfully true, open, and honest. And, that is exactly how we should want our students to be.

> I will be a fourth grader next year. I'm trying not to get Mrs. Redding. Some of my friends' moms are requesting another teacher because she does the same thing all the time and it is so boring. All she does is assign projects where we have to use glue and poster board, you know . . . stuff like that. So, my brother saved his longhouse project in the basement, and I'm just gonna put my name on it and change a few things around. Mrs. Redding is the only fourth-grade teacher in the entire school who gives the same project every year: build a longhouse. It is so funny because my dad said that when he was in school, he had the same project when he had Mrs. Redding! What is with the longhouse? What is so great about the longhouse? The longhouse. The longhouse. The longhouse! [laughs]. I have all of the miniature figurines, trees, and rocks from my brother's. I wish my dad saved his longhouse project from when he was a kid. I could have just

used that one too, unless he got a D or something. Then, there's a bunch of kids in the other classes who are working on building an American Indian reservation using Minecraft. Sounds pretty cool. They are also writing a blog about the incredible history and traditions of Native Americans.
– *Amber Jenkins, third-grade student*

Again, the longhouse project is not a bad thing. The problem with variance, however, is that when the redundant curriculum exists, curbside, and other, more innovative methods for teaching and learning take over, traditional methods might disengage students. Don't get me wrong, some of the best traditional methods of teaching can get some of the best student responses and results. However, in this case, the redundant curriculum is a punch line for students and parents to make jokes about the continuance of a 30-year-old project tradition. Mrs. Redding held on to the longhouse project, mainly, because she liked it. It was a tradition for her, while her students saw it as a sentencing.

What was interesting about Amber's narrative was that it was used as an opening icebreaker activity during an August 2015 new teacher orientation at Robertsville Elementary School. Robertsville had six classroom teacher retirements and hired the most K–5 teachers in history, just last year. Mr. Hughes, the school principal, felt that this would be a great way to help his new teachers think about their practices and methods – while keeping the topic of redundancy at the forefront of their minds. Mrs. Redding retired and was no longer around and the sharing wasn't meant to mock her behind her retired back. But, boy was it powerful!

The orientation was a huge success, and the teachers talked with one another on ways to spice up their own redundant curricular ideas that they were thinking of using from their methods classes and student teaching experiences, which may have qualified them to get the job at Robertsville in the first place. Nevertheless, stories work wonders at Robertsville for this issue and even with issues regarding fieldtrips and recess – which are directly related to student achievement, as well.

Fieldtrips and Recess

Another discussion that the Robertsville teachers had during their new teacher orientation focused on fieldtrips and recess. As sweeping movements to increase recess time across the nation are stirring up much interest and even debate, Mr. Hughes thought that his new teachers should stay cognizant to all of the ingredients that go into positive learning and engagement for his students.

Variance pollutes outcomes when some teachers do something (like capitalize on recess), while others never engage in similar, positive practices. When fieldtrips are used by some teachers, but not others, the learning experiences and potential long-lasting effects of a child's education can most certainly take them down opposite pathways of gathering experiences that their peers might have experienced instead.

Why should some students get one powerful experience and others only end up missing out? This was the debate that Mr. Hughes had with his school board. Funding was a struggle for Robertsville and the PTA couldn't do all the work. Fewer parents were able to contribute their time and money to assist with funding fieldtrips, so Mr. Hughes used narratives and research to make presentations to the school board for funding more fieldtrips across the entire campus so students would have "greater world experiences" (Vascellaro, 2011).

Another factor of variance had to do with the topic of recess. Some Robertsville teachers didn't want to miss out on instructional time, especially with the new state demands and high-stakes tests that would hold teachers accountable for their students' scores. Other Roberstville teachers saw recess as an investment for getting more out of the students. Hence, a little fresh air went a long way for some of the classrooms of Robertsville Elementary, but not all of them.

As a result of these educational debates or issues, Mr. Hughes decided to use some of his students' narratives to ignite reflection for his staff. Below, one parent and one student narrative not only ignited staff reflection during faculty meetings and school planning team meetings, but the narrative regarding recess resulted in 75% of Mr. Hughes' teachers committing to some sort of recess three to four times per week compared to the one to two times per month, which were traditionally used to only "give kids a break," rather than exercise the mind and body as a prerequisite for getting ready to learn.

Both of the following narratives were used in different forums, one for a school board meeting and the other for staff reflection. Both provided outlets and avenues for topics to be digested and analyzed accordingly:

> *My kids used to go on fieldtrips all the time. Now, the Principal tells me that the field trip budget was cut in half due to budget issues. Yet, the District purchases a new math and science program that costs thousands and thousands of dollars. This is the third math program that my middle schooler has had in three years. Why so many changes? Then, they have to buy a new science program because they say that the experimental kits don't meet the new standards. My kids learn more on a field trip than they do in a whole year of science. And they remember the fieldtrips. The whole system is bananas.*
> — Liza Giordino, fourth- and fifth-grade parent

> *Blowing off some steam . . . that's all I want to do. Mrs. Connor's class goes outside all the time . . . even in the winter time! We just sit inside and do double math. I know that adults don't want to listen to kids because we're all just trying to get out of doing school work because we complain that lunch is too short and stuff like that, but I'm serious here. Who doesn't want to get a little fresh air and then maybe we can get through the rest of the day without wondering if we can go outside or not?*
> — Scott McMahon, fifth-grade student

As a result of Liza's narrative, Jeannette Jones, a Robertsville School Board member felt compelled to comment after a board presentation and proposal to increase student field trip funding:

> *Well, you gotta hand it to those who opened my eyes tonight. We sometimes get so caught up in the details of what we define education as books, curriculum, and computers, that we forget what can really drive a student to learn more, inquire, think about the world, and engage in learning within new environments that they may never have the chance to visit without coming to school in the first place. Even though the goal tonight was accomplished, it also grounded me to think about every aspect of student learning*

and affording all students the best experience that Robertsville can offer.

While this chapter is devoted to initiating reflection on topics dealing with educational variance, it provides ways that narratives can offer new pathways for discussion and problem solving through the forums that adults engage in and for the learning communities that can assist with deeper analysis about the decisions that we might be weary of making.

As this book offers direct footing into educational issues, Chapter 4 will IGNITE and highlight how our decision making on how to best utilize student assessments can also have a dramatic impact on student learning and creative problem solving for issues that really need to be busted open.

References

Anderson, S. (2014). *The tech savvy administrator: How do I use technology to be a better school leader?* New York: ASCD.

Askew, S. (2000). *Feedback for learning.* New York: Routledge.

Beninghof, A. (2012). *Co-teaching that works: Structures and strategies for maximizing student learning.* New York: Jossey-Bass.

Brookheart, S. (2008). *How to give effective feedback to your students.* New York: ASCD.

Brookhart, S. (2014). *How to design questions and tasks to assess student thinking.* New York: ASCD.

Cerri, D. (2012). *Classroom instruction that works: Research-based strategies for increasing student achievement.* New York: ASCD.

Curran, B. (2015). *Better lesson plans, better lessons.* New York: Routledge.

Common Sense Media. (2015). https://www.commonsensemedia.org/the-common-sense-census-media-use-by-tweens-and-teens-infographic#. Date accessed: January 12, 2016.

Dueck, M. (2014). *Grading smarter, not harder: Assessment strategies that motivate kids and help them learn.* New York: ASCD.

Marzano, R. (2003). *Classroom management that works: Research-based strategies for every teacher.* New York: ASCD.

Marzano, R. (2007). *Classroom assessment and grading that works.* New York: ASCD.

Marzano, R. (2009). *Formative assessment and standards-based grading.* New York: Marzano Research Laboratory.

Pollack, J. (2011). *Feedback: The hinge that joins teaching and learning.* New York: Corwin.

Vascellaro, S. (2011). *Out of the classroom and into the world: Learning from field trips, educating from experience, and unlocking the potential of our students and teachers.* New York: New Press.

4 Stories that IGNITE Advocacy for Thoughtful Assessment

Education has been in a tail spin for the last few years where parent opt-out-of-testing movements have pummeled the terrain of educational policy making regarding how high-stakes (summative) assessments would be tied to teacher evaluation, remediation decisions for children, and so much more.

Bluntly put, people are tired of the number of assessments students are taking nowadays and although the ESSA Act was meant to replace NCLB in a good way, it is still condoning many of the wrong-headed policies that are directly related to student assessments. Why couldn't NCLB have stood for "No Child Left Bookless"?

Teachers wrestle with how to carry our powerful teaching and assessment that appropriate measures what students know and don't know. They should never have to use assessments, such as those originally created for the Common Core State Standards, where students have no clue about the topics being asked of them on assessments that are meant to help, but only frustrate our students.

So, what are teachers to do? How can they navigate around such insane policy setting? How do formative assessments, quizzes, tests, final exams, AP exams, online PARCC assessments, and midterms work together in meaningful ways, versus creating toxic dead ends for kids?

And, what about the ideals of portfolios, authentic assessments where students create things with their hands, science experiments that are no longer text-based on a sheet of paper during test-taking time, but simply gauged for what students know right there at the lab table without a moment of hesitation from the teacher who knows what to do and when to do it?

This chapter is for educators everywhere who want to see the ideals of authentic assessment and portfolio designs enter back into the field as being the most desirable and most significant tools to gauge student growth and progress. If I had it my way (which I can't), education would be given back to the teachers and school leaders at the local level (and I do not mean the state level) so students can work on meaningful work and be assessed properly by the experts who work with students each and every day.

So, why does this chapter exist if we are talking about the role that stories can play in your school or district or how narratives could be written to tackle issues that we think we can change? Well, we can change the way we think about assessments, and it can all start with powerful stories about what we do each day when we assess students. Take a look at one of the smallest levels of assessment which has been debated for over 100 years in education: the pop quiz. Let's start there (because it is really interesting to check out the following story first, and then we can make our way up to other forms of assessment as we make decisions for how our students will learn the most in the best possible way around! Oh, and don't forget homework too! It is a form of assessment, remember. We don't think of homework as assessment, but it is. It really is. And, it can be incredibly annoying at times (for students and parents). I am not poking fun at you, teachers, but this chapter will help you to continue to wonder, reflect, and change some of the things that you may not even be thinking about. So, go ahead: try out this chapter. I dare you.

Homework and Pop Quizzes, One Century Later

So, how much homework is too much homework? This is an ongoing question that has been posed for centuries. Take a look at the following fifth-grade story that prompted deeper reflection from the staff at the Pleasant Corners Union Free School District in Tennessee:

> *In my friend, Gillie's class, they get homework like every other night, and it takes her about an hour to finish her math and reading. In my class, Mr. Killian gives us homework every night and it takes me like, two hours, sometimes. And then*

> the stuff that I have to do isn't even stuff that looks familiar to me. It's like reading a book written in Russian or something. And math is the worst. We don't even do any sample problems before we get the homework, so how am I supposed to know what to do? My mom is so frustrated because when I ask her for help, she can't even help me because she tells me that my stuff is "new math" and the stuff she learned is "real math." She even got a flyer from the PTA about a math night that my school was planning. She tore it up and said, "If a school needs to train parents on math, then maybe they should look at why they are doing it in the first place."
> – Ellen Andrews, fifth-grade student

This story is not only about the role of homework as being a useful tool for assessment, but it touches upon the issues of variance discussed in the last chapter. Does academic-achievement- outcome-variance exist when teachers who promote a math night versus those who don't promote it impact homework completion results? Ellen's narrative story is chock full of issues and topics for the Pleasant Corners staff to consider. And, that's just what they did:

> If this is just one perception out there about our math program, our students' work load across not just math classrooms, but maybe other subject area classrooms, then there has to be more of these same perceptions, I'm guessing. So, in what ways can we begin to collectively unpack all of these issues, learn more about the intricacies of these issues, and come up with a roll out plan or re-visitation of what we do and why we do it? Then, there is the whole "purpose of homework" debate. Ellen gets "x" number of math problems each night and her friend who has Mrs. Greenhaven for math gets half of "x" each night. We need to better align our instruction with purpose and truly understand what we are assigning students, why we are assigning it, and even revisit what the purpose of homework is even all about?"
> – Barry Caplain, Superintendent of Schools

Setting the stage for reform, Barry led the initiative of "working hard on figuring out what to do with our math program and homework policies."

So, the work began. Barry had a great relationship with his teacher union leaders and, together, they planned on ways to set up grade-level focus groups that would adopt team leaders at each school level within each subject area. Barry even negotiated a stipend for 12 teachers who would facilitate additional professional development on topics related to homework and math program analysis. Parents were also given a free copy of one of John Rosemond's book regarding homework, titled *Ending the Homework Hassle* (1990).

Placing emphasis on growing teacher leaders was the first priority since Barry understood that he couldn't do everything alone. He wanted to keep the trust within the district alive, while also working on decreasing variance and coming to terms with a math program that might not be the best fit for the district after all. See, homework issues and how homework should assess what a student learned on a particular day led to math program variance discussions.

Learning that Ellen's story was not just about Ellen's perceptions, but it also included her mother's perceptions which sparked serious discussions within the district about how the new math program was either preparing students for their state assessments and/or ostracizing parents and students to the point where they might not consider engaging with the schools when it came to curricular matters in the future. As a parent, who wants to come home to a child who can't do their homework and then when asked for help by their child, they can't even help them because the material is much different than the math that yours and mine took years ago?

The point of this narrative analysis is that it took only one student story to prompt self-reflection among staff members at Pleasant Corners to the point where they now are second guessing their two-year-old adopted math program because the narrative from Ellen was aligned with:

1. Poor parent attendance at math nights and other district curricular events
2. Increased percentages of opting-out-of-testing across the district
3. Decreased teacher confidence with math program concepts and rationale for delivering instruction.

Ellen actually formalized everything that the teachers already, informally, felt as they mocked the very math program that their students hated. While narratives offer new ways to look at new issues and provide teachers with professional areas to analyze, rethink, and even reshape, they also expose old debates, while providing new insights into those respective competing epistemologies. Now, let's take a quick look at the role of pop quizzes, another long-standing educational topic that has been debated for centuries, this one also taking place at Pleasant Corners.

> **Wonder**: Do you wonder about what you are "required" to do when working with students and realize that you can speak up, abort, abandon, or throw away poor practices which do not effectively gauge students? We are not talking about doing something that will jeopardize your job; we are talking about punching holes in assessment models that don't really help students.
> **Reflection**: What are three things about the way you assess children that you can reflect on, and if there are things that you have wondered about doing differently, then why not try them out right now?
> **Change**: You can take all of the meaningless stuff that is on your desk and throw it away in the recycling bin. You can focus only on what will give your students the best learning experiences.

"Pop" Goes the Pop Quizzes

In what ways can teachers examine even the tiniest, insignificantly perceived practice, while learning more about the potential effectiveness of their classroom even in these tiny, but, perhaps, meaningful alleyways for helping students succeed? At Lansburg High School, not many teachers give pop quizzes. However, Mr. Lehman, a tenth-grade science teacher, uses pop quizzes all the time, and student grades are posted 20% to 30% lower than in any other science section within the tenth or eleventh grade. This kind of variance has been questioned by the principal, as well. Take a look at what a student has to say about pop quizzes:

> Mr. Lehman gives surprise quizzes all the time. He tells us that it is his way of making sure we read the textbook. I guess I get it, but why are these quizzes worth so much of my grade? We don't really do much of anything else. Couldn't I just read what I want and then prove that I read it? Like with

a project or something? Or work with someone else on the quiz . . . [but oh, no] . . . that would be cheating, I guess. Funny how I learn more when "cheating" than doing somethin' on my own [laughs].
— *Michael Devlin, tenth-grade student*

Here, Michael is upset about pop quizzes, but there are more issues that sparked collaborative sharing among the science department staff at Lansburg which included:

1. Defining the role of the textbook and textbook usage
2. Examining how to increase project-based learning
3. Revisiting group work versus traditional definitions of cheating
4. Creating increased social learning environments versus individual learning tasks
5. Streamlining the weighting of assignments and their overall impact on cumulative grades.

What was most effective about this narrative tool was that when Michael approached Mr. Lehman with his concerns, Mr. Lehman transcribed what Michael said to him and as a result, he used Michael's concerns to reflect on his own teaching practices while also taking the narrative to a science department meeting. Mr. Lehman didn't buck what Michael was saying. He didn't act hard-headed or rigid. He didn't step away and say, "I'm your teacher; I know best." Michael's points and Mr. Lehman's narrativizing of Michael's points became a win–win for everyone – even Mr. Lehman's future students in years to come who haven't met him yet.

There, a discussion was born on the five factors outlined above and now, today, Lansburg engages in increased cooperative project-based learning where students carry out hands-on experiments to illustrate their understanding in both chemistry and general earth science concepts. Students are more engaged, grades have increased, and student participation has increased. The textbook is also being used as a support, not the main vehicle for instruction or compiling student grades. Ever read *Ditch that Textbook* by Matt Miller?

So, there's homework and pop quizzes. There were narratives that triggered wonder, reflection, and change at Lansburg. But, what about all of the other types of formative and summative assessments that students either love or hate? How can stories be used to trigger reflection even though we may have already thought about some of these issues, informally, when talking with colleagues in the hallway or during faculty meetings? The topics presented in this book are not rocket-science topics. But, the point is: narratives turn informal debates into formal debates. They pack punches that we cannot ignore. They embrace what students feel, and we should never ignore what our students feel.

Popsicle Sticks

You know what I'm talking about: popsicle sticks with students' names labeled on each one as they sit in a jar or coffee can on a teacher's desk. We all know about that formative assessment tool. It's been practices for years. I'm not even sure who came up with that, but we have seen an increase in educational supply companies coming out with quick, catchy, and even more innovative tools for teachers to gauge students, right there on the spot, to catch a glimpse into what students know and don't know.

But, did you catch the words, "on the spot"? Look at what Shelley, a fifth-grade student in Georgia, shared with her teacher, verbally, before her teacher, Amy Hathaway, took Shelley's words and narrativized her discussion with Shelley and shared it at a department meeting that was based on discussing formative assessment tools which would be used across the school as a means for gathering authentic feedback from students:

Shelley: Miss Hathaway, I . . . I . . . have to . . . well, I . . . need to tell you something.
Amy: Sure, honey. What is it? You look like you've just seen a ghost.
Shelley: I . . . I don't like . . . well . . . I . . . I just don't like answering stuff in front of the other kids.
Amy: Oh, I see, honey. Is that why you looked so upset and didn't even look at me when I called your name?
Shelley: Uh huh. I . . . I just don't . . . see . . . I just don't like that popsicle stick thing that you do.
Amy: Well, maybe there is a way that you and I can work out an agreement. I won't pick your popsicle stick and make you feel uncomfortable, but how about if you keep this small index card on your

desk, and as I walk around looking at everyone's work or asking questions to see what your classmates know, you can place your answers on the card, and I can just glance at it when walking by to see if you understood the math concept. How about that?

Shelley is just like so many other students we've met: shy, unsure of herself, and even embarrassed. And, we know that's okay. This simple dialogue between Shelley and her teacher illustrates nothing new to us. But, what if, just what if, this narrative triggered a reminder to other teachers to remember our shy students as we take flight in so many different kinds of extroverted formative assessment activities? What if writing replaced speaking for Shelley and her comfortability increased and then directly resulted in higher achievement results because she was no longer scared about having to talk in front of her peers?

Sure, we can stand back and feel that it is our duty to try and move Shelley into a zone of being able to speak up in front of her peers, but sometimes, we cannot force a bull into a compact car. Sometimes, we have to simply arrive at where our students are, take heed to how they learn best, and even though a goal might be to help Shelley to speak up in front of others, Shelley's reality in the here-and-now is that she is just timid. She's not a low ability student. She's just timid. And, we have to take our students' words for where they are right now. In fact, it took a lot of guts and bravery for Shelley to speak up and talk to her teacher after class. That, in itself, illustrates that Shelley felt comfortable enough to talk to her teacher – which is a hats-off admiration that we all should have for Amy.

So, to her department meeting, Amy went, and as she shared this dialogue with her team members, the teachers thought about ways in which their own constructed formative assessment tools could address two types of students: those who are extroverted and those who are introverted. This is how the meeting proceeded to be set up for future meetings, and it was through this one simple, captured, narrativized dialogue that the students at Amy's school would be better served.

Amy could have gone into her department meeting and said, "Hey everyone, don't forget about our shy students when we think of compiling a list of formative assessment tools." Of course, she could have simply done that. But, Amy's narrative packed an emotional punch for the other teachers and a few of them even had an emotional response of, "Aww . . ." Plus, Amy decided to keep a copy of her dialogue with Shelley in her purse to always remind her about the terrific students that she gets to work with each day. Amy and Shelley had a special bond. That's what using authentic stories will do. Create bonds.

Writing Portfolios

We often think about authentic assessment as being anything other than pencil and paper tests. The power of writing is re-entering back into education, not just as a means for preparing students to take tests that include short answer written responses or extended essays that are test-based, but rather journals or portfolios that truly invite students to get their thoughts down on paper. Writing goes hand in hand with reading, and the mere creation of creative text is when we might stumble across the next big idea that our students come up with.

But, how does writing work at your school? What does a good writing program look like? How can we wiggle our way out of not only using writing to address the Common Core Assessments, but so that students will want to write even when they graduate from high school? These are tough answers to provide, but there is one thing that the research presented in this book *does* know: writing has the power to transform student learning in ways that we cannot possibly imagine. Take a look at the story below from Efram Rodriguez, a director of curriculum in Florida:

> *We looked at the writing practices of 50 teachers within two of our high schools in the district and analyzed the types of writing that took place over the course of two consecutive school years: 2013 and 2014. Through our analysis, we found that 75% of the students who kept journals and writing portfolios of their favorite written pieces scored higher on the Florida Assessments than the students who didn't keep journals. This is astounding to us in so many ways. We know that students are different in each of our class years, but this kind of number is not a fluke. I really believe that. What this information did for us was to analyze the types of writing that the teachers who used journalizing and writing portfolios used and how those practices could be replicated across*

all of our high school classes. There still is a lot more for us to analyze, but one thing is for sure: creative writing, journalizing, and writing about what students want to write about is still very alive in our district. While using the Florida Assessments is not always a good gauge because it consists of so many narrative nonfiction writing tasks, there is something to be said for how creative writing or daily writing simply increases writing fluency and that is something that we need to do more of.

Efram realizes that writing, in general, is a process that should be replicated, not just so students do better on their summative assessments, but that writing, in general, is something that should be valued more than it is in their current instructional program. Often, we get so caught up in the role that multiple-choice questions play with succeeding on tests or exams that writing may very well take a back seat to more mundane tasks where student interest may very well decline.

So, this story doesn't do much in terms of telling us something different than we already know. We know that writing is important. We know that creative writing shouldn't die. We know that journals are effective ways to get students to open up and write about whatever they want. Right?

It is the power of where this story went next, which is incredibly interesting. Efram is a delegate and consultant for the State Education Department in Florida. He shared his own narrative with the department and was able to win a grant that would fund a new writing program in his district to be used as a pilot study for analyzing the total writing program and the results that were found across the 50 teachers that he originally studied a few years ago. As a result, some grassroots professional organizations and parents formed writing centers in Florida where further studies were going to be conducted. While results are preliminary and there is still an initiative for writing analysis to be carried out, Efram's summary narrative was used to trigger discussion. It helped others to wonder, reflect, and potentially change the way writing was being taught, the way writing was meant to be, and the way writing could, ultimately, open up eyes as to what students were doing each day. That is about as authentic as one can get: authentic stories about authentic practices is something that we can analyze each day as teachers and school leaders.

Wonder: Do you wonder how one story might lead to an epidemic or ripple effect of something that you discover as an educator? Do you wonder if there is something that you will learn by looking at just one slice of your educational program?

Reflection: Can you think of three scenarios or components of your curriculum where assessments are linked to some other more powerful form of learning? Can you think of ways to capture data and narrativize your own story or findings so that others can learn more about creating a more effective program that doesn't strictly rely on tests, assessments, or quizzes, per se?

Change: You have so much information in front of you as a teacher or school leader. You can grab one element with tweezers and examine it to see if your hypothesis about something leads to greater student achievement.

Test Construction and Preparation

100 in 40 or Fail

We have all heard this story, as well: a teacher creates a 100-question test that students are supposed to complete in 40 minutes. The students who cannot finish become frustrated. They start to hate learning, test taking, multiple-choice and matching activities, and ultimately don't even know what to do with the 63% that they might receive on a test where 25 questions were left blank because time ran out.

How are assessments being used in your classroom, in your school? In what ways do we feel so tied with having to assess students in the traditional ways that we do because we are driven by summative assessments from the state level? In what ways do we abort poor practices and expose them for what they are: poor? Can our own authentic stories ignite change? Can we collectively agree that practices, such as this, are wrong-headed? Below, Mary Sommerton, a principal in Pennsylvania, shared the following story with her staff as she humorously put a ban on wrong-headed assessment practices, such as those described above:

> *If I want to buy a car, I don't go to a motorcycle store. If I want to buy a dog, I don't go to a hardware store. If I see*

> that the speed limit says 65, I don't drive 105. Unless I'm crazy. If I want to connect with my students, I don't do things that will upset them. There once was a teacher who gave a 200-question test in 30 minutes. That teacher could have been sent to the hospital if her kids were old enough to drive because gosh, it would hurt to get hit by that 105 MPH car!

This funny script went viral around Mary's town, not because she decided to turn it into a press release or something like that, but because her staff was talking about it for weeks. They still laugh, to this day, about Mary's funny approach to using a simple narrative to unite her staff on an issue related to assessments that could have driven a wedge between those who carry out such wrong-headed practices with those who wouldn't even think of testing students in that manner.

While the faculty laughed at such a funny story, a few teachers in the crowd certainly sloped in their chairs, knowing that their practices may have been aligned to that which we feel is wrong-headed. Either way, confronting the issue set a standard in Mary's school – a standard where assessment was no joke, should never be unfairly created, and should always strive to engage learners. Mary realizes that multiple choice is a fact of life. She didn't advocate for a ban on multiple-choice questions. What she did was steer reflection down new pathways for her teachers to think deeply about every assessment that they give, every test that they construct, and that photocopying sample tests out of teaching guides is never an authentic or powerful task for anyone.

Read that Packet

We have also seen or heard about the teacher who creates a study packet that is 30-pages long and gives students one week to study before a test. They reassure students that if they study the packet, they will have everything that they need to know and more and do quite well on the upcoming test. But, what happens when a student actually writes his or her own letter to a teacher as a means for advocating for other students and himself or herself? What happened to Sarah Jablonski, an eleventh-grade student in Ohio, when she rigorously studied for a test, but found out that while taking the test, something else happened, instead? Take a look at what I think is an incredibly mature way to handle a concern even if Sarah decided to write a letter to her teacher instead of talking to her, directly. I think it was the power of the cc: that Sarah wanted to use as leverage for getting to the bottom of something that not only upset her, but wanted resolution to for herself and for her classmates.

Dear Mrs. Goldberg:

I am writing to you with respect, not revolt, but I am very concerned with something that just happened to me. I'm sure it also happened to my classmates, as well, but I thought I would come to you, first, before freaking out and causing drama with them. I studied your packet last week and actually memorized everything before today's test. I knew the content like the back of my hand, but when I took your test, there were about 30 questions that had nothing to do with what I learned. I also know that those 30 or so questions were not in the study packet that you gave us. The topics did have to do with U.S. Government, but that's about it. I feel that this is unfair and I wanted to bring this to your attention as you grade my paper and everyone else's paper. Why would you steer us in one direction only to turn the wheel in the other direction at the last minute? I chose to write to you instead of coming to you, directly, because I wanted my mom to not be upset with me if I get a failing grade because of how the test really wasn't fair to us. I hope you won't now be mad at me because I wrote this letter to you. I still like your class and think you are a cool teacher. I just wanted to speak up, not only for me, but because I'm wondering if my friends are also going to get failing grades on this test if they studied the packet that you gave us and the promise you made that if we knew the packet, we would be fine.

Sincerely,
Sarah Jablonski, 3rd period
cc: Mom

In this case, a letter was constructed as a form of advocacy. The power of this letter and outreach at Sarah's school is unknown, but for this book, it is a story certainly worth mentioning. Students who write and narrativize their own thoughts are just another example about how authentic stories can ignite wonder, reflection, and hopeful change.

Wonder: Do you wonder how Mrs. Goldberg reacted to this letter? What about Sarah's mom? This study never followed up with Sarah, but one would hope that Mrs. Goldberg's reflection was triggered as a result. I'm confident that there was no punitive retaliation against Sarah, as well.

Reflection: Have you ever given students a task that they never learned just to see what they know and don't know before moving forward with teaching a new concept? That's not a bad thing. But, have you ever given a task to students that wasn't really fair on an assessment? How else might you assess student learning in your classroom? Do you use the same tests each year? Do you use the same assessment procedures each year?

Change: How you assess students is just as important as what you assess. Try changing just one thing that you currently do by trying a new assessment technique.

What we do with our assessments can make or break our students' backs. Assessments that are unfair, wrong-headed, or lack creativity can wind up damaging the relationships that we try so hard to positively establish with our students. Assessments can wind up unwinding everything that we discussed in Chapter 1. Do you want to ignite or frighten your students? Do you want to wonder and reflect or ponder and deflect? You can be the change, and all it takes is one simple story to IGNITE others to change, too.

Reference

Rosemond, J. (1990). *Ending the homework hassle.* New York: Andrews McMeel.

5 | Stories that Make Us Wonder about Our Own Policies

Our own policies and practices with how we teach, how we expect students to learn, and how we assess students can be examined through authentic stories or narratives, indeed. But, can stories also be used to ignite wonder, reflection, and change regarding our own policies that are set up in all of these areas? Of course they can.

When we dig our heels into our own policies, offer little to no flexibility with policies that really don't make much sense as to why they were written in the first place or why someone wrote them, we set up a huge wall between what we believe we must stick to our guns about and what others perceive to be "crazy" standards.

We've all seen it before: a teacher, leader, committee, school, or district sets a policy. They don't think of all of the ways in which that policy will be implemented and someone comes along with an issue that makes the policy that we created look silly. We either become defensive about our policy (because we created it and view anyone who questions our policies as being an adversary), or we make a decision to amend, rewrite, or update a policy that we agree is silly.

The problem with policies is that policies can easily tick people off, especially when we hear others say to us, "Well, that is our policy." Yuck. I've heard that a million times and as a former school administrator, I remember looking at policy manuals and thinking, "Why in the world do we have this policy?" or "Oh my God, this policy hasn't been updated since 1990 and it doesn't address modern day issues!" The problem with policies is that we know we need them, we are governed by them, but they are these set-in-stone things that we know we need to change, but we sometimes just never get around to changing. They help to establish hopeful order, but they also can be the same types of policies that upset others or make us crazy!

Well, the good news is that authentic stories can get others to see the insanity within our own policies and policy making even though I'm not saying that you should go to the superintendent's office and burn all of the policy manuals. Here is what I contend: wonder, reflect, and change anything that gets in the way starting right now and cause your change movement by using stories. Remember, they pack a punch and IGNITE others to either revise or get rid of the educational garbage that sits around everywhere in our schools.

Policies that are Silly

We all have them and I'm not trying to be petty with this section, but students tell me all the time: "This (policy) just doesn't make any sense." We don't mean to upset our students and the policies that we set are supposed to strengthen safety and discipline, but sometimes we go a bit overboard with our localized policies. Take a look at Tyrone's story below and notice how upset he is about something that he feels is just so senseless:

> *The hall monitor is insane about hall passes. If you don't have a hall pass, she cooks you. She does. She electrocutes you. She should be working in a jail somewhere. With prisoners. Not kids. So, I came down the hallway after coming from the lav and not feeling well. My teacher told me to just go to the next class and he didn't give me a pass. Then, Miss R. saw me coming. I thought, "Oh God, I don't have a pass." She gave me such a hard time. Like I was trying to run out of the building or something. All I was doin' was just going to my next class. I didn't feel all that good, so I snapped at her and that landed me detention. But, she wouldn't stop. She kept going on and on about not having a pass. I couldn't take it anymore. She rode me and then I snapped. I know I shouldn't have mouthed off to her, but she wouldn't listen. Now, I have to miss practice after school because I have to sit in a hot room all because I didn't have a pass.*
>
> *– Tyrone Blakely, tenth-grade student*

We create policies to protect students, but does this scenario go overboard? The policy is, "No student is allowed in the hallway without a hall pass that is visible." Did Miss R. stick to her guns insomuch that it drove Tyrone crazy? Tyrone gets blamed with disrespect *and* not having a pass. What did Miss R. think was happening after Tyrone explained his situation? Do we assume that students are lying to us and always up to no good? Silly. This situation should have never happened.

Then, there's Marguerite's story which points to another policy that could, perhaps, be silly too. I'll let you decide. Check it out:

> *If I don't have my binder in class, I lose 10 points for the day. But, Mr. Ewings never checks to see if we have it. The thing is so heavy. I have to lug it around. Papers are popping out of it because it is so crammed. And by the end of the year, you can't even stick anything into it. We don't even use it, really. It's just there as a reference, I know, but couldn't we just know when we need it and when we don't? I decided, yesterday, that I wasn't going to bring it. Samantha harassed me like I was committing a crime. And would you know it: Mr. Ewings checked to see if we had our binders! Just my luck! And Samantha was laughing so hard that I just broke down and cried. Stupid binder.*
>   – Marguerite Mendez, sixth-grade student

Being prepared is one thing and it is important, don't get me wrong. But, does Mr. Ewings' binder policy really help students to learn and achieve? Does the loss of 10 points do more damage than good? Do we set policies up to gather some sort of compliance standard? Do we clobber kids over the head with what we think is a really good thing, only to find out that it upsets the very students we are trying to win over? Silly, perhaps. Minute, these policies may seem. But, sometimes, these policies automatically turn off our students, especially if we are only satisfying what we think is important – which really might not be after all.

Policies that are Missing

While policies often upset us, there are also instances where the lack of policies make us just as crazy. The problem with policies is that sometimes, you never can win. You may jeopardize relationships along the way when either implementing a policy or creating a new one. Most likely, when policy revisions are made to already existing policies, committees are established to come to agreement with what is best for students and the community. But, even then, revised policies have the power to shake up your relationships for the worse. Take a look at Dwight Hoover's story, shared all the way from Alaska, about his desire to establish policies for PTA purchasing in the district when donations are made with good intentions:

> *I need to work more closely with the PTA because they purchase things on their own without me knowing and then when I find out that there is a smartboard or interactive whiteboard being installed in a classroom, it is missing cables, a projector, and so many other parts-and-pieces that it, then, costs us more money to purchase individual solutions instead of a package that could outfit the entire board for about $500 less. Don't get me wrong, I am grateful for the PTA fundraising and everything that our parents do, I just need to be more involved so we can save money for the school district and keep better records of what is being purchased, with what money, how it is donated to the school district, and where the receipts are in case we are audited.*
>
> *– Dwight Hoover, Assistant Superintendent of Business and Administrative Services*

A loss of funding for schools across the nation continues to be a problem. While some states tout that state-aided funding has actually increased, the overall expenses of educating a student has also steadily increased over the past five years. For Dwight, writing grants, fundraising, and carrying out systematic procedures for fundraising management has added additional hours on to his 60-hour work week.

Working with various district and community committees on how to increase revenue for the district is a difficult task, but ideas have been generated for parents, teachers, students, coaches, and school leaders on how to best maximize resources for their school district by way of seeking classroom mini-grants or larger scale fundraising – while also staying true to keeping corporate America out of the messages sent to students through anti-sugary-sweets and anti-soda vending/fundraising campaigns sparked at many local levels.

Dwight's narrative was used at a School Business Officials Meeting in his local regional area, and it spread the discussion of initiating protocols for fundraising management into other school district regions, as well. Today, the majority of school districts near Dwight have created sound management practices for fundraising prowess, and a major collaborative study group has also been set up so Dwight's colleagues can work together on strategic plans for fundraising, together. Various books are being used in Dwight's study groups, as well.

As you can see, even central office administrators and leaders can grab hold of current events through narrative analysis to move professional learning and problem solving to new heights, both locally and regionally. Issues of resources, budgeting, and money are a high priority topic for school leaders across the nation, and stories can be used to construct new ways of learning, sharing, and problem solving about topics that we stumble upon or have thought about.

> **Wonder**: Do you wonder about any policies in your school or district which have upset others? Have you questioned why a particular policy was created in the first place or how you could create a new policy for your classroom or school that can address an ongoing problem?
> **Reflection**: Can you think of one thing that you can do starting tomorrow that will revise a wrong-headed policy that doesn't protect or advocate for students?
> **Change**: You can share an authentic story with your supervisor, principal, superintendent, or school board about a policy that needs to be confronted or created.

Policies that Leverage

Sometimes, policies that we feel are already "set in stone" are used to move our platform forward. Sometimes, this works for our students; sometimes, it backs them up into corners as we demand them to do certain things. Earlier, we talked about strict homework policies that had no flexibility for students. We've seen other educators "grade" student behavior. Is that fair?

Other, larger, landscape policies, such as those created by school boards or enforced by superintendents start to become blurry as the political field is mined to move ahead with plans, desires, or dreams. Take a look at how a superintendent in West Virginia worked through his own proposed consolidation plans by using policies that leveraged his motives:

> *We need to close schools. Period. I don't care how much push-back I get from parents or the community. Our enrollment is declining, and no one has stepped up to alert us to logical ways to save money aside from cutting personnel which is already a given. As a result, it is my job to move forward with what is best for the district even if it isn't a popular decision. We need to re-design the district and in the absence of advocacy for the taxpayers, I need to assert my power. We even have a policy that outlines class and school size and authorizes our board of education to make decisions on closing class sections or schools.*
>
> *– Gavin Ormsby, Superintendent of Schools*

There is much to learn from Gavin's narrative – how policies can leverage decision making, but something else that was very unique existed with the creation of this simple story: Gavin Ormsby's narrative was used by the Superior Lake Central School District Board of Education during a new superintendent search. The narrative was used as a recruitment tool where applicants needed to respond to the text and touch on ways that this text "spoke" to them. It was a leadership exercise, one where there would be right answers and one where there would be wrong answers for the candidates speaking with the school board members.

The board of education members didn't like the top-down leadership tone displayed in the narrative and screened applicants within the first round of interviews by using this narrative to seek desired and undesired responses using the methods outlined in my first breakthrough book about using narratives, titled *Hiring the Best Staff for Your School: How to Use Narrative to Improve Your Recruiting Process* (Routledge, 2016). Superior Lake was faced with declining enrollment and needed to take action for a major redistricting and school closing plan. As a result, Superior Lake used narratives as tools to hire the best superintendent whose values and attitudes matched what they desired in a new school district CEO.

Together, the board of education members held study sessions for their own professional learning regarding methods to use for hiring a new superintendent of schools, along with reviewing professional literature that assisted them to understand school closing procedures, conducting enrollment studies, and the importance of communication and public relations strategies for rolling out a comprehensive plan for the district that wouldn't leave Superior Lake divided or angry because rational solutions were not provided to the community.

See, stories can be used in every part of education and at any level, as well. Stories leverage outcomes and mine for attitudes and dispositions that we wouldn't otherwise realize.

Policies that are Abused or Taken for Granted

Policies also govern timelines and deadlines. We all know that. Tasks or responsibilities that provide us "30 days to respond" or "15 days before a sunset clause kicks in." We've seen policies enter into the legal field of human resources, but we also see them govern teacher's deadlines for handing in student work. This is not always a "bad" thing, but then there are those who use policies to their advantage. Notice how the following narrative written by a parent in New York raises our eyebrows to a very basic timeline policy that we've all heard of before –Committee on Special Education procedures:

> *I had to call the school to see when my CSE meeting was going to take place. It has been like forever when I wrote a letter to have my child referred to the committee. I needed help writing that letter in the first place and even though I wrote it in a few minutes, the school district dragged out the entire process for exactly 30 days. When I called the principal, he told me that they are within the law. All I said was, "That's the amount of time you have to comply with the law, not the amount of time you just automatically take while my son struggles."*
>
> *– Gloria Evans, parent*

What is interesting here is that Gloria makes a good point. We know that educators are super busy, students are on waiting lists to be tested, and counselors have enormous case loads of students. Administrators have to clamor around to prioritize the thousands of tasks that they have each day and parents, sometimes, see education only from the outside. Should a 30-day deadline automatically mean that we take 30 days? Do we strive to beat our own policies if it means helping a child now rather than later?

These are the kinds of questions that stories elicit: wondering about something that we can streamline, do differently, or reframe, insomuch that we can stand tall knowing that we don't just become automatons to policies that have already been established. We can push ourselves to do better. We always can.

> **Wonder**: Do you know of any kind of policies where deadlines might hurt children? Do you wonder about what you can do to change that?
> **Reflection**: Think of one policy that you know of or have created and then reconsider your policy with a fresh, new, rewritten version that advocates for children.
> **Change**: Policies are not set in stone. They aren't the 10 Commandments pounded into tablets. You can change or recommend changing any policy that governs any part of education – whether it is classroom based, school based, district based, or even state based. Your advocacy and voice can help to change anything that is already in place.

Policies that Protect

Organizational design through policy creation is a reality of each and every single school district in the nation. We evaluate staff members based on policies, contracts, or agreements. School boards, for example, have an incredible duty to hire superintendents. In fact, that is probably their number one task aside from having a fiduciary responsibility to the taxpayers and overseeing school budget creation and adoption.

In the case of the Greenfield School District's responsibility to evaluate their superintendent of schools, like every other district where the board must conduct the evaluation, something strange took place, and a parent's narrative sparked enormous debate. Check out what the issue was:

> *The parents are revolting against the district. They have had it with the superintendent. No communication. No personality. The teachers are beside themselves. They live in an environment of fear. The superintendent visits classrooms and criticizes everything. She never says one positive thing to anyone. But, the board just extended her contract. What do we do with something like that? We elected the board and then they go and do whatever they want to do without getting any community input that we heard them promise to us when they ran for office. I don't feel like anyone ever tells the truth anymore. How can we entrust our students' welfare in the hands of liars?*
>
> *– Jessie Owings, District-Wide Home-School Organization Vice President*

The Greenbrook Central School District had a mutiny on its hands. The board of education and superintendent were divided against the community due to differing opinions about the leadership in the district. What once was a peaceful district based on trust, positivism, and construction, quickly turned to a district that was based on fear, dishonesty, and destruction. The board policy for evaluating the superintendent did not have any language that community input would be used. In fact, it was widely known that the board president and the superintendent regularly hung out together on weekends and holidays. They became good friends.

About 50 miles from the Greenbrook Central School District, Lisa Connors, Evansville Central School District Parent Teacher Organization President, decided to use Jessie Owings' narrative to bring about a sense of unity within their school district as a new board of education election was quickly coming in the springtime. Lisa used Jessie's narrative to hold "meet the candidate nights" and set up a district-wide committee that would reconstruct the district vision, mission, and goal statements for the next five years in Evansville.

Jessie Owings' story was the cornerstone of creating a proactive plan way before campaigning and elections took place. It was through the use of story that Lisa Connors creatively used one story to paint a picture of what she did not want to happen in Evansville. The community rallied for the best and brightest board of education members to be elected and those who would work closely with the superintendent on creating positive plans for the district, while also holding them accountable for their actions, behaviors, and promises. And, their board policy was overhauled to include a series of stakeholder surveys that would take feedback into consideration versus strictly being used as the evaluative tool for their new superintendent.

It is no secret that politics and community relations are realities of most schools and districts across the nation. We have all seen spots of positive and negative politics at play and as a result, action through told stories or narratives can help organizations to learn and grow in new and amazing ways.

Debates about having lavatories for boys, girls, or students who are transgender will force districts to institute policies about even this one hot topic. Sometimes, policies are a no-win situation. Sometimes, they come back to bite you from behind. Other times, it is up to us to take our old policies, dust them off, and figure out the very best ways to service students.

> **Wonder**: Do you wonder about something that your school is dealing with right now where there is no policy or guideline to frame your decision making? Do you wonder about cell phone policies, no-hat wearing policies, dress code policies, or anything else in between that effect students?
> **Reflection**: Can you look at your own school handbook or policy manual tomorrow and examine it for fairness, inclusiveness, and clarity? Is it good for kids?
> **Change**: Dust off that which hasn't been dusted off and seek a new mindset for policies which may, inadvertently, serve students poorly. Be the change agent that they need even if policies seem so far away from what you can be doing in the classroom as a teacher or in your school as a leader who will IGNITE everyone through stories.

Stories that IGNITE policy reflection can be very helpful to educators. Then, there are *politics* that creep in to classrooms or schools and such politics are sometimes hard to ignore. But, stories can counteract negative political influence or even build up a toolbox for combatting the inevitable politics that certainly exist in our schools today. Chapter 6 will provide a lens for how stories can shield us from politics or drive us to new frontiers that will help us to wonder and reflect about the very nature of the existence of politics and what it really means for our students.

Stories that Help Us to Work through Educational Politics

Politics made the top seven categories, which can either act as a detriment to schools or IGNITE new ways of thinking or pushing back on a system that has already and can potentially further damage children in the future. Politics are a pain. They are distractions to things getting done. They are mosquitoes that fly in your ear – nuisances that upset us or hold us hostage to poor methods of doing business or running an organization. They are paperwork laden, annoying, but also a fact of life.

To shake up politics, slow them down, or just simply divert them, stories IGNITE the wonder, reflection, and change necessary for organizations to stay alive and thrive in amazingly powerful ways. Educational politics can exist in all types of forums: local, national, or international. Sometimes, local politics beat us up the most because it involves things happening right in our own backyards. Yet, national politics always have the power to affect our local lives and this is where this chapter will begin. How does the Common Core IGNITE your organization to wonder, reflect, and change ways of doing things in your district?

Common Core Politics

We all know that various legislators and leaders at both the national and state levels acknowledged that the implementation of the Common Core Learning standards misfired, broke the speed limit, and gathered so much negative press and publicity due to the roll out and expectations set forth in the new literacy and math standards. Tied directly to the Common Core assessments, which were then tied to teacher evaluations, the Common

Core State Standards have combusted into one of the biggest political forums that education has ever gone through.

Expectations for teaching our students new ways of thinking, text complexity, and higher cognitive analyses of literature, problem solving, and word problems have evoked school leaders and teachers to purchase new programs that are aligned with the Common Core and even create new positions within their districts, causing parents and community members to question and second guess administration as being a "voiceless body of suits who carry out political agendas which do not advocate for children," said Gretchen Darrow, a parent in New York State.

Stories have battled against Common Core politics, such as stories of children feeling hopeless on Common Core Assessments, principals who do not know how to best support teachers when there was little to no direction across implementation phases of the movement, and parents who automatically rebelled against the Common Core when they took a first look at their children's homework assignments which were being brought home.

School districts across the nation have created new positions within their administrative ranks to attempt to support teachers with the Common Core curriculum and new packaged programs from some of the nation's largest publishers. Recess has decreased across the nation at rapid rates, and children are continuing to become frustrated with the politics that drive such reform movements.

I'll bet that we can all agree on one thing: reform and making education better for our children is a common priority, and we all do have the best intentions for helping our students to succeed. Yet, our voices are often "silenced" when we deal with the realities of having to move forward with the Common Core and find only minimal salvation in packaged programs which promise to raise scores or give the best outcomes versus their competitors. Big business is big business, and stories have grabbed educators by the collars for giving them back the voice that they feel has been lost.

Please keep this in mind as you read this section and the one that follows, which are related to the topic of the Common Core: I am not exercising my opinion about the Common Core in this chapter; I am demonstrating how stories chipped away at a national, political movement that is still taking place today. Stories IGNITE and they prepare anyone within the educational system to use them as flamethrowers.

Now, take a look at how the following stories were used in Ohio, New York, and Pennsylvania:

> *I have two masters degrees and over 16 years of experience as a fifth- and fourth-grade teacher. I know how to teach literacy, but also work hard to keep up with new methods that will best help my kiddos. But, when someone tells me that I'm no good. That I'm a washed-up teacher who only knows older curriculum constructs, my mind starts to simmer and I start to boil. All of a sudden, I'm not adequate to teach my students, and all of these new administrators in my district to carry out APPR and Module coaching – which came from Common Core demands – start to strangle me and make teaching something that I never signed up for. It is so sad what I see in the classroom. Developmental activities placed on younger students end up going right over their heads. Yet, I'm the dumb one. I'm the fool. Politics in education is the monkey on my back and the nightmares that these students face when they become equally frustrated when they can't do something that I am now supposed to tell them to do.*
> – Rachel Bings, teacher

> *Our district just hired a Module Coach. I cannot believe that taxpayers are footing the bill for yet another initiative that is supposed to support the Common Core. Has anyone added up the dollars spent on Common Core support? No. No one has. Administrators hide that reality and the ones with spines try to speak up, but the political machine from the top-down just squashes them like bugs.*
> – Cathy Evans, fourth- and ninth-grade parent

What politics does in these two cases is to IGNITE anger. The problem here is that politics can elicit so many deeply rooted emotions that it might be unfair to those who must plot along or do their jobs or the jobs will be in jeopardy if they don't show results. Politics create positioning where sides are set up: administrators versus us. Teachers versus them. And, the result is a faulty level of what we want to do to IGNITE others to tackle the issues that are more important for our students. Teachers feel inadequate. They feel deprofessionalized. All because of new curricular movements? Maybe not. All because of the politics which drive new movements? Maybe so.

Politics get in the way. They just do. They bend us. They take us away from more important things. They transform us into werewolves and make us feel inadequate. Politics drench us with buckets of water, inadvertently, hoping that we will drown (or at least, just conform). Earlier, we talked about how variance kills quality. Well, so does conformity. To conform means that we will not look for increasing quality.

So, how can stories bring out the positive aspects of what we need to do to IGNITE wonder, reflection, and change in our system that is still overrun by Common Core politics today? How can we craft stories that will move us forward with enormous advocacy for our students?

We can see such movements related to the Common Core, such as the opt-out-of-testing movement, which has national implications. Later, in this chapter, you will see how stories became the backbone of how this movement got steam. All from our stories. All from our hearts. Stories IGNITE passion.

The Common Core State Standards and "New" Math

A subset of the Common Core politics is the new Common Core math curriculum. Using new methods of problem solving in order to rethink math concepts became one of the major criticisms of those who know their basic math facts versus those who lost such skills by zeroing in on, exclusively, Common Core problem-solving strategies. Programs such as Eureka Math came along and touted an irresistible offer (not guarantee, of course) that such a program would lift students' math scores. Notice how stories also brought about mathematical persecution when parents all across the nation complained that they were helpless at helping their children at home due to the new ways of thinking about math.

Another debate related to this one is that parents shouldn't have to help their children with homework. Is it or isn't it the child's responsibility to do their homework, and if they do not understand something, they should report to their teachers for help? Here is where stories IGNITE reflection on this issue and drive others to deeply consider why we are doing what we are doing, and why we are still searching for answers well after the Common Core has been here for years?

> *Across the nation, school districts are setting up parent training sessions so we can learn how to help our children with math? Are you kidding me? Why doesn't anyone see this as a red flag? [sarcastically]. "Oh, yes, Miss Parker, come on in for two hours over the span of three different training sessions so we can show you how to do math with your child. We also have the answer keys to all lessons on our website in case you get stuck. This is a great way to ensure that your child will progress in math." It is so unbelievably insane! Since when are parents supposed to be coming home from work to do homework? I opted out of state testing anyway, so why can't I opt out of the math program that the school adopted to raise these test scores? [laughs]. Hey, wait a minute . . . that's not a bad idea! Jeez. What ever happened to flashcards, memorization of math facts, and solving a subtraction problem without using lines, circles, sticks, or whatever they tell the kids to draw! Or, just giving students just the right balance so they don't leave school only thinking that they have to measure things using paperclips! Since when does adding three-digit numbers to another three-digit number result in using drawing sticks and circles on the paper, rounding up, and then adding the number only to subtract that which was rounded in the first place? Insane! The whole thing is insane!"*
> – Sarah Parker, second- and fifth-grade parent

Unfortunately, stories, used in this way, only set up others to sound like they do not "get it" or are just complaining. However, I am contending that the more we use stories, document them, narrativize them, and share them, we are collecting gasoline bonus points to fuel the cars of advocacy for our students. If there is a movement, any kind of movement, that we feel is not in the best interest of our students, then nationally and locally we have a right to voice our concerns. And it is when stories are captured and used that the greatest change will occur.

Stories and Educational Politics

The Opt-Out Movement and High-Stakes Tests

Earlier, I mentioned the power of the opt-out movement where parents and educators (even students) banded together to refuse Common Core assessments. For reasons tied to these tests driving teacher evaluation to the roll out of the Common Core to the implementation to our programs which cost taxpayers millions of dollars, the Common Core stumbled a bit because of our stories. Voices have been heard, new contexts for communicating with administrators have been created, and even principals have smiled at the traction that gained so much steam within the Common Core political opt-out movement. Here are just two of the millions of stories which elicited and provoked reflection and change under the Common Core movement:

> *The Commissioner of Education recently announced that she will be reducing the amount of time that students have to sit for state assessments in all grade levels. Do not be fooled by this ridiculous bone that was thrown to us or our students and give up the fight that we, as parents, must continue regarding opting our children out of the unnecessary, stringent, and ridiculous state testing. This is just another slap in the face for students. Keep fighting the good fight!*
> — John Michaels, fourth-grade parent, New York

> *I watch my kids take these [state] tests. They look horrified when they take them. Some of the kids break down and cry because they can't finish. There is anxiety in their little faces. We spend so much time getting ready for these tests. Now the new buzz word out there is "grit." Do your students have enough grit to sit for these tests, persevere, and concentrate? I'm kinda glad that so many parents are opting out of the testing movement. I don't even know how it really impacts my "score" as a teacher, but who cares? I only have another four years to go and then I'm out of here.*
> — Gretchen Phillips, third-grade teacher, Ohio

Sadly, teachers want to retire, policy-makers become the enemies, but reform takes place with such advocacy through storytelling and narrativizing the words that come from our hearts.

> **Wonder**: Did you ever wonder how not getting involved in educational politics only ends up involving you, by default, anyway? How did that happen? What were the circumstances to you (accidentally) becoming involved? What did you do in order to deal with it?
> **Reflection**: What are you doing today with your curriculum that you can do differently tomorrow? Did politics drive you to do something in a way that you really don't like doing? In what ways can you advocate for your students so that what you do is not a by-product of politics, but a creative way for you to navigate through politics?
> **Change**: Common Core politics is just one example of how educators and parents have spoken up for what they feel is right for students. Are there any other politics in your organization where you, too, can speak up about to further advocate for your students or staff?

Follow the Leader through the Chain of Command?

Another major political facet of the educational system which educators and parents, time after time, have shared with me as I collected stories for this book is the issue of "following the chain of command."

What kind of silly world do we live in where no one can have a differing opinion about a topic or issue – especially when schools plot along each day, sometimes doing the same things it always does? In what ways do we insulate ourselves and place the monkey on someone else's back so we don't have to deal with something that we don't want to deal with?

Chains of command are sometimes necessary for categorizing areas of expertise. One would not ask a teacher to speak about the oversight of a capital improvement project plan where faulty electrical circuits were installed within the ceiling panels. That would be the clerk of the works' job. A physical education teacher should not have to be concerned with the legal bills of the district or carrying out *foil* requests that just came in. You get the idea.

But, what if chains of command set up walls for us and limit progress? What if we cannot open any door to the walls that are set up – which only exist to simply resist? Take a look at how one parent called her school superintendent to find out about an issue:

> *All I did was call the superintendent because her director of student services wouldn't call me back. I get the whole chain-of-command thing, but if one person is dodging me, why wouldn't I climb up the organizational ladder in order to get an answer? I just wanted to know why my son's special education program was no longer going to be offered next year and what my CSE process was going to look like regarding recommendations. I went to the principal first, and he didn't know. So, that's why I tried to get some answers elsewhere. But, the moment I do, I'm labeled an enemy or a trouble-maker. I mean, c'mon. Why is the system set up like this so that I'm in the dog house because I'm asking questions? I'm nice, not mean. I value administrators. I'm not anti-superintendent. But, stuff like this makes me wonder about how much longer we are going to be treated like anarchists. Something's gotta give.*
> – Bev Gibbons, sixth-grade parent, Missouri

We spend so much time creating organizational charts for others to follow. Certainly, this helps with understanding who is in charge of what area of expertise. But, organizations often use this chart to their own *disadvantage*. We get so stuck on who should be doing what or who is responsible for what that relationships might suffer as a result. Stories can be used as ways to get back in to a situation that we might be told to stand outside of until someone is ready to address our concerns. Meantime, students might suffer, topics might go unaddressed, or issues might be forgotten. Narratives remind. Narratives remember. Narratives unstick something that is stuck. Stories IGNITE others to take more care or have more attention to something that we are not paying attention to.

Bev's story was shared at a PTA regional representative meeting where other parents talked about strategies for communicating with administrators. While the anonymity protocols that I outlined in Chapter 1 were not used by Bev (because everyone knew who her superintendent was), it was the inaction of the superintendent that led to this narrative being shared in the first place. So, Bev didn't care if others knew about who the superintendent was at hand within this real situation since she was more concerned with getting resolution for her son.

Sometimes, narratives might make educators look bad, but only if a story is falsified or shared, knowingly, that there would be a breach in confidentiality. In this case, Bev's superintendent shot herself in her own foot by not responding to Bev and only referring her back to the director of student services who didn't respond to Bev in the first place. In this case, Bev was getting the run around, and her story was used to promote change, not anarchy within her school district or regional discussions with other parent leaders.

> **Wonder**: Do you wonder what would happen if you didn't call any of your parents back or try to resolve any of their issues? Do you wonder what would happen if you were a principal and referred everything back to your assistant principal or nurse? Do you wonder how parent conferences would go if you blamed parents for the lack of student achievement? Of course, all of these situations have many stories behind them – years of expertise or experiences that illustrate educational victories or struggles.
>
> **Reflection**: In what ways might you reach out and change your current system so open communication or forums filled with open-mindedness can flourish even more than you already think they are? How can stories be used to bring others together even when times are treacherous? Can a negative story help you to gain positive footing for change?
>
> **Change**: Politics can sometimes frustrate us and bring out the worst in us, but it is within those experiences of political frustration that we can build better bridges or question our role in sustaining political machines that can make students' lives more enjoyable and productive in the classrooms and schools that we lead.

Questioning Decision Making

Many of us have been taught since a young age that questioning adults is disrespectful. While there is some truth to this statement, there are also some falsified implications behind such a belief statement. As a child, questioning a parent could be disrespectful. However, we have taught our children to respectfully question anything that doesn't seem fair or right. So, when do topics in education like this exist, and what is the best solution for anyone concerned with education to be doing about something that they think isn't right for their school or good for students?

Take a look at one school district in Michigan where the new superintendent would not only enforce distancing herself from her organization in order to be insulated from hot topics, but how her school board members would shun those who would speak their minds when they told their stories:

> *I am calling for the district to re-examine the school consolidation plan and give voters a new opportunity to decide how our school district will function in the future. I am also calling for the consolidation plan to be delayed for one year so that parents, staff, and the community has a better chance to prepare for whatever the voters determine and make arrangement with proper details given to school administrators, teachers, and parents sooner, rather than later, about the new plan. Just because a plan was approved by previous administration does not mean that it is immune to a new review process by the new administration.*
> *– Jessica Jennings, second-, fourth-, and sixth-grade parent*

After the board of education meeting ended, Mary, one of Jessica's friends stayed back to ask one of the board members a question. Without thinking that Mary heard one particular board member poke fun at Jessica's public comment, Mary left quickly and decided to not stick around after all.

Frustrated with how parents were being treated in the district, Jessica's story did not halt the consolidation plan in her school district, but what did take place was a "shake up" with how the parents in their district would no longer stay silenced about issues just because the superintendent or board "said so."

Jessica left the school board meeting when it ended and found no resolution to her questioning the district's plans. Her story was ignored by the school board, altogether, and no one made a comment or responded to

Jessica, as well. Not even a "thank you for speaking up" or "we appreciate your concerns." Nothing.

What Jessica's story did, however, was to garner more support for parents sitting in on district planning committees. It also demanded that such committee meetings would be held at times where parent representatives could attend the meetings. Typically, planning meetings were held during the day when staff members could attend, but for parents who worked the first shift, as well, many could not attend and assist with the decision making that was going to take place.

The Race for a School Board Seat

It doesn't sound like running for a school board seat should influence or impact what you are doing in the classroom or your school and most times, it doesn't. Yet, there are lots of times when it does. Running for a school board seat means that a particular community member, often with one or more children in one of your schools or who has many friends in your district or community, is going to run a political campaign. And, yes, children, teachers, parents, and school leaders are affected in one way or another.

Even though teaching and learning is always the number one focus, school board races are still political races and the platforms that a particular member runs on can often times be in question. Below, you will find a myriad of reasons why school board races are both political and emotional and have emotional impacts on the entire community in some shape or form. Does a school board member run because of any of the following?

A candidate might want to:

1. Be helpful
2. Volunteer because they (now) might have the time to do so
3. Change an issue or program that they are upset about
4. See a school leader, teacher, or another employee no longer be in their position for a host of all sorts of possible reasons
5. Take some sort of action through the avenue of a hidden agenda
6. Assist a family member looking for a job

7. Help children (sincerely)
8. Use a school board seat to leverage a larger career in politics.

There are other reasons, too, of course.

So, how can stories assist with driving, exposing, or protecting the political terrain that actually does influence all of us in a community? How can stories protect that which needs to continue taking place each day (teaching, learning, and fostering children to do their best)?

Educators have shared with me that school board elections actually do impact their teaching and leading because it is a political race that they cannot simply ignore. The students whose parents are running for a school board seat could be susceptible to a bullying incident if their parent is not liked. A teacher's spouse may be running for a seat on the school board and that, in itself, sets up a whole other series of implications. Maybe a friend doesn't like the superintendent, or a tax payer's group promotes a particular board member because they want to see the budget be defeated. Maybe a school board member is running in order to activate some sort of revenge.

Stories can uncover or quiet down a situation. Take a look at how Jeanne Frye, a PTA President in South Carolina, used a story to unravel the true intentions of four board of education candidates who were running for just one vacant seat in a 2015 election as she ran a "meet the school board candidates night" at the high school of her district. Her introduction to the community, which was already embroiled in a political battle, provided everyone with a "take the bull by the horns" attitude that set the stage for the night to take on a powerfully different tone that was not expected at all. It was potentially going to be hostile, until Jeanne set the stage in this way:

> *There are rumors, at least I'm hoping that they are rumors, where our community has learned that there are some wrong-headed reasons for why particular board member candidates are running for our school board in the first place. I want to communicate to our community that our school district is committed to making sure that our students are not affected by adult interests or misbehaviors. We are here for children, not platforms which are unaligned to our intent on making sure that our kids are safe, well educated, and don't*

> *fall victim to adult politics. During tonight's "Meet the Candidates" session, it is our job to ask the tough questions, and although any one of our candidates can choose to give us a different answer than they know is opposite in their heart, it is within the spirit of democracy that we make well informed decisions instead of decisions filled with rumor or fiction. We need to heal our district and not hurt it any longer. Our students hear us, see us on the news, read about us in the paper, and shouldn't have any distractions whatsoever. I caution everyone in this auditorium to put forth a professional and amiable attitude so that we can decide, as voters, on who is the best fit for leading our school district.*

Here, Jeanne roots for civility and her story sent a shockwave of professional demeanor for getting everyone on board before the "fireworks began."

While this one story acts as an example for helping to establish a professional forum, one might wonder how school board members could also use stories to illustrate their intentions and positions. Can we tell others about the deepest thoughts and emotions that are on our mind so that politics do not jeopardize the community in any shape or form?

> **Wonder**: Do you ever wonder how a story might help to make someone do something differently, such as changing procedures or including others to speak or sit in on a topic? Do you ever wonder how we might be upsetting someone by our status quo mentalities?
>
> **Reflection**: Is there a time where you may have purposely, or inadvertently, tried to silence someone? What was the issue? How could you have handled it differently? Did the issue place a wedge between your relationship with that particular person? Could you have offered different guidance or input that would have helped move a moment forward, rather than end up going backwards?
>
> **Change**: You don't have to enable politics or become a politician to survive in your career. Speak up and stand up. Challenge and be challenged. Model innovative thinking versus going with the flow. Put the brakes on any locomotive that you think is impossible to slow down or stop. Why not try? Why not use stories to pack a punch as you IGNITE others to change any situation that needs changing?

The next chapter is a chapter that will keep you celebrating all of the great things that you do on a daily basis for students or staff members. And, within the field of narrative theory and how stories can IGNITE classroom and school change, motivational stories are the very best types of powerful communication tools that bring out the best in everyone: teachers, teacher leaders, principals, assistant principals, and superintendents.

# Stories that IGNITE and Motivate Teachers and School Leaders

You've seen it before: a teacher reads a motivational story or quote to their students. A principal reads a poem or motivational story to their staff members to get them pumped up for the school year. Pleasant notes are placed in mailboxes. Teachers leave tokens of appreciation on their students' desks. We all love being built up. We all love being loved. We pull stories from everywhere. Motivational quotes are all over Twitter and LinkedIn. Facebook posts are funny and positive. Storytelling is the center of how we communicate with one another and even though there are research studies about the power of intrinsic motivation, we still love to be extrinsically motivated.

Who wouldn't want to have a mother who tells you that she loves you while growing up or even as an adult? We want to be needed. We want to feel appreciated. And, education is often times a field filled with unappreciation.

Can stories bring us together? At what point do motivational stories lose their power over motivating us? At what point do stories become saturated in our capacity for wanting to feel appreciated? Well, I can't answer those questions. What I can do is report to you that the teachers, principals, and other educators that I have worked with for so many years absolutely love hearing about stories filled with victory, heartfelt appreciation, or stories that illustrate battling unsettling conditions that turn a happy ending. I've never heard of a teacher or principal overdoing it, being too lovey-dovey. But, that's not what this chapter is about. I don't want to recommend overdoing anything.

Yet, something tells me that teachers and school leaders, collectively, have these inner emotions of why they went into education in the first place. I did and I still do. When I hear stories about students tackling a problem, overcoming pain, or experiencing joy in the classroom, it does tug on my heart strings. We *all* have heart strings. Board members. Superintendents. Teacher Aides. Counselors. We all do.

So, why would stories of motivation or educational passion actually *reform* organizations? Well, they have a direct impact on establishing a culture of caring, and while I could take the time to cite research and bore you to death with proving that this is so, I'm not going to do that. Instead, I'm going to share some of the stories that have been used in schools across the nation which help teachers to wonder, reflect, and change the things that might drive them crazy or distract them from doing what they do best on a daily basis.

Based on the stories that educators have shared with me in person, through my website, or via my online survey, I've categorized them into two major sections that will pack a punch for triggering wonder, reflection, and change. They are Stories of Victory, and Stories of Defeat. Yes, even stories of struggles and defeat motivate educators (in reverse) to rise above the ashes and strive to come out on top. Humans have an innate sense of searching for stories that talk about darkness to find the light, because we are all humans and these human types of stories do so much for us when we feel like quitting, giving up, or not crossing the finish line with whatever we are doing. But, first, let's start with stories of victory that capture the essence of what we strive to do with our students each day.

Stories of Victory

We wake up each morning to change students' lives for the better. We are in this business to make a difference. We want to IGNITE others to do their best. Take a look at the collection of stories that illustrate victories across the nation. These stories come from all sorts of stakeholders in our classrooms and schools and the stories, themselves capture the spirit and heart within all of us.

I pulled stories from different types of people to demonstrate how we really do have a collective power in building on our victories and trying our best to replicate success. Fasten your seatbelts, grab a box of Kleenex, and celebrate, with me, all of the great things that you do:

> *Cassidy hated school after the first week. I kept getting phone calls from Mrs. Simmons, her teacher, about how Cassidy*

started throwing things in class. Crayons. Papers. Even a stapler. This wasn't like Cassidy. At home, she never threw temper tantrums. Now that she goes to kindergarten, all of a sudden she is a monster? But, this didn't phase Mrs. Simmons. Not at all. It was like she was immune to these kinds of things. These kinds of behaviors. It was so interesting to me. She was the calming force that got Cassidy to simmer down, control her emotions, and be constructive, not destructive. Mrs. Simmons could have thrown Cassidy out of class, but she didn't. She worked with her. She talked to her. She cared about my daughter and created a victory for Cassidy. Kindergarten can be tough for lots of kids, but Mrs. Simmons gets the prize. She is absolutely a magician. I don't know what she did, but patience, caring, and lot of love made Cassidy excel. This is a celebration story of Mrs. Simmons. This is what teachers do each day and we often don't know all of the moving parts that they balance and orchestrate. This is a story of victory. Simple as that.

– Sheila Dawson, kindergarten parent

I'm not gonna give up on any kid. Ever. My heart goes out to all of my students who struggle each day. Being an urban teacher has its advantages and disadvantages. The advantages are that my life becomes meaningful because I help the most challenging students who have incredibly sad home-lives and realities that I cannot even possibly imagine. The disadvantages are that I think of them all the time and they tug on my heart. I guess that's not really a disadvantage, but my life is dedicated to my kiddoes. I love them. I will never let them down. They will not fail my class, either. I will follow them home if I have to. I will read to them at night if I have to. Nothing will stop me. Nothing.

– Latoya Brown, third-grade teacher

We can either be office robots or social beings. The paperwork, e-mails, and phone calls will not go anywhere. They will always be there in the evening. My students go home at 3:30, so all of that other junk can wait. Being a principal isn't paperwork to me. It is being in my students' lives. It is walking around and talking to my students. Just the other day, I found myself doing something in my office that I didn't want to do: organizing the state assessments into piles that needed to be placed in the safe. Writing down lists of students who were absent and needed to come down tomorrow for re-takes. Comparing last year's scores to the initiatives that we are tackling on our building committees. Then, I dropped my pen and decided to walk away from my office. I just went down the hallway like I was sleepwalking. I needed to see students. It was like I smelled a turkey dinner and followed the scent or something. I ended up in a kindergarten classroom. There was a substitute teacher who looked like she had her hands full. I sat in the class and helped. I noticed Emily was shivering and she had her hand raised. The substitute didn't see her hand, so I went over and asked Emily what she needed. She just wanted to go to the coatroom to get her sweater. That's it. Sweet thing. What a great girl. It sounds like this wasn't really a big deal, but for Emily, she couldn't concentrate because she was cold. It is through those small victories, how we pay attention to children that makes me proud to be a principal, not the junk on my desk that really is meaningless in the grand scheme of things.

– Jeff Kramer, Elementary Principal

Jeremy needed to gain a few more pounds and he was so obsessed with doing so. I mean, the kid was really obsessed. He was binging like crazy. I wasn't pushing him to do this. He was. He wanted to qualify in a different weight range and go after one of his long-time rivals with the Panthers. I started to see Jeremy get a bit out of control. What started out as a joke between us, got a little weird. I think Jeremy was starting to get a bit unhealthy because of his obsession. He even asked me about steroids one time. That raised a major red flag to me. So, I took Jeremy aside one day after practice. I don't know what I said that day. I cannot even remember what I said, but I spoke to him like his father would have spoken to him. I didn't mean to. I just did. See, Jeremy's father passed

away last year from a heart attack. It was super tough on Jeremy and his mom and little sister, so getting a scholarship for wrestling was Jeremy's #1 goal. But, he was trying to get there in a real unhealthy way. I took Jeremy under my wing and worked with him every day after school and after practice. We would eat dinner together, too. I felt Jeremy in my heart. Yeah, I'm a big dude, but I still have a teddy bear heart. I really felt for that kid. I felt like it was my job to not just coach Jeremy, but to encourage him to do things the right way. The healthy way. He could have gotten real sick at the pace he was going. Real sick.
– John Hawkins, varsity wrestling coach

I started using heroin two years ago. I knew I had a problem. It was tough to stop. When I couldn't get a fix, I would steal money from my grandma to get back on the high that I needed to stay on just to function. If my grandma didn't have any money, I would take something of hers and sell it. Or, I would get creative [clears throat]. *Believe me. I wanted to stop, I just couldn't. Until Mrs. Jennings grabbed me in the hallway and pulled me into her office. She knew about my addiction because Harmon told her. I wanted to kick his ass, but I didn't. Looking back now, I knew he did it to help me. Mrs. Jennings get me the help I needed. I've been clean for six months. I'm doing OK in school too. Yeah, I sometimes get the craving to pop a shoestring on my arm and shoot up, but I know how to deal with stuff now. I know I'm a fighter. I wouldn't be alive to tell you my story, I think, if Mrs. Jennings didn't help me. She was my angel. She will always be my angel.*
– Jasmine Pitts, twelfth-grade student

These stories of victories are game changers. They remind us why we went into education in the first place. We deal with so much each day because our students deal with so much in their lives. We get up in the morning to help our students. We would have it no other way. We are, collectively, human beings who were meant to help others. We have a calling.

So, where could stories, such as these be shared? If you remember back to Chapter 1, stories, like these, can enter in to so many different areas of your daily work. Whether a superintendent uses stories at graduation or when conducting a keynote to teachers who use stories to pull up their students who are working through a difficult task to parent leaders using stories in order to illustrate good program decision making as they support their schools through PTA events or the like, stories have the power to unite and reunite. Plus, how could anyone discount good news and victories?

Sure, we can tell others about the victories that we had or we can show them in print. Either way, stories trigger us. They just do. Stories capture the heart of education and they bring others together to a common feast. Stories exude power and create powerplays for us in our classrooms and schools. It is hard to refute that stories are the best research out there and act as medicine to heal us and drive us forward. Storytelling through narratives is not fictitious or some strange form of psychobabble or voodoo. Stories are real and they mean business because we are real and mean business too.

- **Wonder**: Do you ever wonder if you would get different results during a meeting, assembly, or school function if you just took a minute to step back, ignore the agenda for a minute, and kick off your gathering with a story that would bring you all together with great clarity, focus, and passion?
- **Reflection**: Where could you use a powerful story to share with others and motivate them to greater heights? What should you tell your colleagues, students, or parents and which story will trigger them to feel like they just got a B12 shot from you?
- **Change**: You can use stories to send powerful themes and plotlines throughout everything that you do. Your story will help someone to become motivated. Capture a story right now and share it with someone who feels down. Share a story with someone who needs a boost today. You have a duty to help others, and sharing a story is sometimes the best medicine.

Stories of Defeat

Should we teach our students about defeat? Should we treat defeat as an avenue for victory that is just delayed? Should we openly talk about defeat in our faculty meetings, department meetings, and curriculum meetings?

What about talking about defeat during orientations, parties, or anytime we have an audience in front of us? When we collaborate with others on any topic in education, we can either ignore the stories where failure exists or we can IGNITE others to embrace failure or defeat as we search for solutions or new ways to get different results. Take a look at these stories which testify defeat. Then, look at how these stories were used to grow allies, tackle adversity, or reframe old ways of thinking and doing.

> *I don't really like the person I've become. I can see my ego getting the best of me. I'm starting to make decisions by myself and calling it shared decision making: where I make a decision and share it with others later. I never used to be this tightly wound when I was a teacher, and, hell, even while I was a principal. But, the stress of trying to be everyone's problem solver for things that I'm not sure I can even really solve, is getting the best of me. I know I'm not liked. I know that you make fun of me, too. I know that my contract probably won't be renewed because I've created so much opposition with you. I know that. So, it is really hard for me to stand up here and read this narrative to you. I'm not looking for sympathy from you. I'm just asking you for your forgiveness. I really want to do better. I do. Let's try it out. Let's start working together and I will promise to start treating you like the professionals you are.*
>
> *– Josh Pryor, Superintendent of Schools*

Josh shared this narrative and read it out loud during his end-of-the-year staff meeting which was one year away from his final year as superintendent. It took a lot of guts for Josh to say these things, let alone write down his feelings. Sharing this story was not a planned tactic for getting another year on his contract. In fact, Josh didn't get an extension on his contract, but what he did do was learn more about himself as a leader. He soon enough landed on his feet and found another school district to lead further downstate in Arizona, and he is doing quite well today. See, Josh's story is about as open and honest as one can get. And, even though Josh left the district that this story was shared at, his staff respected him as a result of Josh respecting them. If that is not a powerful story, then I don't know what is.

But, just down the road, in a different school district, Mitch Campo, a school board president read the following story to a packed audience at his final board of education meeting which led to his resignation as school board president. Notice how Mitch's story of defeat helped his community to heal during a time of political unrest:

> I'm having second thoughts about being elected as School Board President. I've thought long and hard about what I wanted to say to you tonight and I want to share something with you that I am wrestling with. I ran for this school board with the wrong intentions. At first, I wanted to help the students of this great district, but then I lost focus. I ran for the board and sought the support of the community who was upset with our superintendent. But, as I see everything that Ellie does on a daily basis, I have built such a great respect for her. I cannot sit by and become a minority member of this board who has a revengeful platform for getting rid of someone that I feel is doing a great job. I think Ellie is misunderstood and I don't expect you to believe me, because many of you don't. Being a superintendent is a hard job that many people don't ever want. It is a thankless job. It is high profile and stressful. I don't envy what Ellie has to do each day. But, I cannot lead any further attacks on Ellie. I can't and I won't. Some people have called me a fool for turning back on my platform. I don't care. You are going to have to find another president that will take down Ellie. I won't contribute to it. It is with this spirit that I now make a motion to resign as a school board member, effective immediately, and am asking for a second to this motion, please.
>
> – *Mitch Campo, School Board President*

From school board presidents to superintendents to students, stories have healing powers even if they are stories that share our own defeats or losses. When we crash and burn or think that we aren't doing a good job, our stories can live on to teach others about the human spirit and everything that we stand for in education. Stories also help us to do things *right* or to set things *straight*. In the case of Mitch Campo, he was no longer going to contribute to the attacks being made against Ellie, his superintendent of schools. Narratives that illustrate our defeats can turn defeat into victory. Mitch walked away with his head held high because he knew that his own defeat was better off being turned into setting an example and living by principle – one that he would carry with him from that day forward. The community learned a lot from Mitch taking a stand, as well.

I give students a lot of credit, too, when they share their stories. Take a look at this powerful story from an incredibly articulate young man whom I admire because I don't remember being this mature as a sixth grader myself:

> *I didn't do what I was supposed to do. I didn't stick up for Bobby. I let him sit there and get made fun of. My mom didn't teach me to be quiet when something is wrong. She taught me to stand up for myself and to stand up for those who can't stand up for themselves. And, I let it happen. Richie kept riding Bobby. He kept calling him names. Right in front of me. I should have done something. I mean, I didn't laugh at what Richie was doing, but me keeping quiet is just as bad as laughing at Bobby, anyway.*
> – Jake Perkins, sixth-grade student

Stories can help to motivate us and help others to see things that they might not see. They have the power to help others through similar situations. In this case, Jake's story was shared with the students at his middle school with his permission. He wanted his name to be placed on his story. Certainly, Richie and Bobby's names were protected by pseudonym.

We all have stories to tell, and if we don't tell them, we decrease the potential of triggering wonder, reflection, and change. We might be embarrassed or are not ready for deep reflection, but why not share your story and give it a try? At every level, sharing something that gets in our way can have amazing impacts on helping us to think in the reverse and then move forward in a new direction. We are creative human beings. We are educators.

Recognizing the Conditions for Celebrating Educators

Are there times when you or your colleagues are down? Are there times when you need a pick-me-up? Are there times when we work so hard for our students that we just flop on the couch at night, totally exhausted from what the day entailed? There are conditions for administering "B12 shots" through storytelling and you have the agency to recognize those conditions and assist your colleagues with trying your hardest to make them feel like a million bucks. Here are a few quick tips about setting up purposeful contexts for defining the conditions where stories can motivate your colleagues and peers.

Your use of stories, to motivate others, can be used when:

1. **There is a sense of defeat in the air.** (Ex. Your superintendent reports that your assessment scores dropped by 5% as a school even though you know you worked harder than ever to help your students achieve.) Stories that carry on the torch for passionate teaching are appropriate to share.

2. **Things seem stale.** You know what I mean. It is those times when Spring Recess can't come quickly enough or the snow starts to turn black and you just feel plain yucky as a school or classroom of students. Stories ignite us to "shake it off" and to continue celebrating the beauty of our profession.

3. **There is something to celebrate right under our eyes.** These aren't just birthday parties, but maybe a teacher received their NBCT or Ph.D. Maybe they finished a course that was difficult, or they took on a leadership role in their union or in the community. Maybe your colleagues stepped up and set up a new club for students. We have so much to be thankful for, and often, we forget to celebrate all of the *great* things happening that we don't stop to recognize.

If we have a calling, as collaborative educators, that permits us to share our worth with one another, then how can we teach our students that their *own* stories can actually help their classmates and teachers too? It is in this spirit that we finish with Chapter 8, which focuses on how students write stories to help other students and educators just like Jake's story helped his school. Chapter 8 will be brief because it is part of another book that I am currently writing for you, titled *Stories from the Playground: How Students Write Narratives to Help Adults Solve REAL Problems in Schools.*

Did I IGNITE you to wonder about this concept some more? Good. Turn the page for more.

Stories Written by Students for Helping Other Students or Adults

What if our students rose to the task and carried out a call for action that we empower them with by using stories to help their peers and us to wonder, reflect, and change anything in our classrooms or schools that needs changing? What if we treated students as problem solvers where the tool of narrative writing could activate and trigger powerful outcomes for schools?

I am not talking about having students write dead end business letters to companies or about causes that we want them to become involved in or creating personal letters where students try to persuade the principal to lengthen their lunchtime. What if students were tapped on the shoulder to tell us about what *they* experience so we can make their lives better, easier, or more meaningful? What if students were given autonomy to create and recreate new ways for us to think about the system of education in which they reside? Can it be done? Is it silly to think so? But, where is the research behind this idea? Do we need research to prove that stories can transform classrooms and schools?

The stories that educators share with me and my colleagues to spark and IGNITE us to do better are remarkable. And, there are students all across the nation who are writing to their teachers and their principals about *real* things – stories which pack and then unfold their feelings and emotions for us, adults, to better understand. These stories are not at the end of a survey instrument, either, where we try to collect student perceptions about all sorts of topics or initiatives going on in our schools. No, this section is more than fulfilling a business letter writing unit or looking for ways to merely collect perception percentages about canned topics that we think our students care about. It is more than trying to persuade a principal to extend lunchtime by 15 minutes.

As we teach our students about writing narratives, in what ways can we redirect our instruction to carry out just two powerful questions that could be posed to our students:

1. What do you (students) think that we (educators) can learn from *you* (students) about your daily life as a child or as an adolescent who is growing up and developing into a young adult?
2. What are *we* (educators) missing when we think that we (educators) know better than you (students) do?

Makes sense?

Teaching Narrative Writing

There are many teachers who teach the art of narrative writing by starting off with graphic organizers that will assist students to collect and organize their thoughts. This is a proven best practice tactic in education, but for this chapter and in my next book, I'm contending that we do something different.

For narratives to become emotionally charged – you know the ones that will be a few paragraphs long – and the ones that will truly IGNITE us to start wondering and reflecting about a topic, students have to do three things:

1. Be mad or glad about something
2. Tell it like it is (use emotion and true feelings)
3. Record what they *really* say about a topic and then narrativize it, afterwards (transcription is okay; it is actually a powerful learning tool and skill).

That's it! I'm serious.

Take a look at some of the stories written by students that were meant to help other students and adults to wonder, reflect, and then drive changes that are based on their own ideas and perceptions about something that made them mad or glad. Look at what types of topics emerged when students thought about school, their education, and the daily victories and barriers that they face each day – their *real-life* experiences and advice to us that is embedded in what they say to us.

Boys Will Be Boys?

> *Big deal, so a few of us guys were messing around in the locker room. We always put our pads on and run into each other like sumo wrestlers. We aren't picking on the smaller kids on the team; we are just having some fun. Why can't kids just mess around without everything always being called, "bullying." It is so stupid how my teachers and principal are so hyper about everything. They need to take a chill pill. I mean, really. Lighten up. They probably did worse things when they were kids. No one is going to get hurt and this isn't hazing, either.*
> — Evan Rogers, twelfth-grade student and captain of the football team

Evan's narrative raises some incredible points for us to discuss. What is bullying? Is everything bullying? Is there such thing as "boys will be boys" or "kids will just be kids" *or* have we failed to address situations that should be addressed and teach our students more about why we are addressing something? Does there need to be understanding between students and adults about what hazing is? Could someone get hurt?

Evan invites us to wonder more about what he really means. Sometimes vague stories pack a punch for helping us to see so many different viewpoints. Can a school analyze this narrative to IGNITE some study questions on how to address bullying?

Posting Student Work (a Story in Reverse)?

> *My teacher posts our work in the hallway. So do other teachers in my hallway. Essays, projects, you know, stuff like that. But, there is always someone pulling down our stuff. Kids walk by on their way to lunch and rip stuff off of the walls.*

> *So, what is the use of putting anything in the hallway, anyway. I mean, who is gonna stop, read my essay, or look at my project, and be like, "Oh, that is really cool. I loved the metaphor that Emily used in that essay" [laughs]. I can understand open house night and parent conferences to make the school look good and make parents proud, but what about the kids? Maybe we could learn from other kids' stuff? Or, why is it there in the first place, then, like all year long? And, why does Mrs. Gillian put new stuff up on the walls each month just so it ends up on the floor?*
>
> *– Emily Devlin, fifth-grade student*

Does Emily's narrative cause us to wonder more about why or why not we post student work in the hallway? Do we reflect on what our students know about exemplars? Mentor projects? Mentor texts? Model homework assignments? Do we teach our students about the role that taking pride in our own work and someone else's does to overall student achievement and building a positive school culture? Do we teach the "rules" of brainstorming so no idea is ever labeled a dumb idea? Do we track what we post, whose work is posted, and how it helps others? Is our daily hallway traffic so busy that we just pass right by student work without ever stopping to truly take the time to appreciate it beyond its simple appearance of dressing up our hallways?

The Never-Ending Discipline Cycle?

> *I've kind of had it with the jerks in my class. Jacob, Johnny, and Russ always mess around, get into trouble every day, and I can't even get my science experiments done because they take all the materials and throw them around. When they get sent to the principal, they just come back to class after a time out or detention the next day. Why can't they be suspended or something else? They are taking away from our learning. Mrs. Owens gets so mad at them and has hall passes with their names already printed on them even before they come into science class. The moment they breathe wrong, she gets them out, but they just come back the next day and do it*

> *all over again. So, my friends and I decided to take matters into our own hands. Like 10 of the kids in my class cornered Jacob, Johnny, and Russ after school and told them that we were sick of their crap. Even Emily, who is the prettiest girl in the school, told them off and those guys have a crush on her, so it was kinda funny. We cornered them and will keep cornering them since no one else can get these idiots in line.*
>
> *– Sarah Peters, seventh-grade student*

How do our students feel about the principal's office or the time out room? How do our students feel about the trouble-maker? How to we empower our students to nonviolently have them monitor one another and build each other up (even while appropriately policing one another)? Are we, as educators, quick to throw out a student who misbehaves? How do our students perceive everything that we do? They are always watching, you know.

What about My IEP? Creating Students with Voice

> *I know I have an IEP. I know what I need help with each day. I know my own weaknesses and how I can make my learning stronger if I get the help that I need. But, what happens when I don't get the help that I need? Well, I become frustrated. I mean really frustrated. I couldn't get my special education services all last week because the district had some teacher training going on, and there weren't enough substitute teachers to fill in. So, they pulled my special education teacher to cover other classes and now I can't do tonight's homework because I had no clue what to do. When are my administrators going to pre-plan for things like this and make me a priority?*
>
> *– Kathy McGovern, seventh-grade student*

Kathy's narrative is unbelievably metacognitive. What do our own students know about themselves? What do we take for granted that we think they don't know? Do we include them on our decision-making teams and planning teams? Do we ask our students what they think of something that we know is already a problem in order to help us realize that something might be an even bigger problem than we realize?

Master Schedules from a Student's Perspective?

> *I guess music isn't important anymore. The superintendent made all of the principals take music out of their schedules because we are supposed to take longer math and English classes during the day. "It'll help the kids' test scores," he says. So, now I have to get up at 6:30 in the morning, get to school by 7:30, and my dad has to drive me there before he goes to work just so I can take Band. I love playing the saxophone, but now I have to do it so early. I'm half asleep. Then, when I get home after taking the bus, it's like 4:30. When I have baseball or football practice after school, it makes for an even longer day. I am just exhausted the next morning and don't even want to get out of bed to do it all over again.*
> – Joey Cattucci, seventh-grade student

> *I get up at 6:30 a.m. every morning. I'm barely awake. I grab a Pop Tart if I'm lucky and then my bus picks me up. First period is a joke. So many heads resting on the desks. I'm usually still tired, myself, from the night before because I worked at the restaurant bussing tables so I can save up for a clunker and take Allison out to the movies without having to ask my mom for her car anymore. Why do we start school so early, anyway? It is so stupid. Half of my friends don't even come. They get to sleep in and still pass their exams because they are somewhat smart even if they don't study, at all, for anything.*
> – Josh Michaels, twelfth-grade student

Can students tell us what is important in *their* schedules? Can *their* narratives help us to analyze our own district and school schedules? Can our students' narratives help us to reflect about what we are doing? Can our students compel us?

See, the common thread among these stories is that students wondered and reflected about what they do and what we do, as educators, each day. They tell it like it is – whether they are mad or glad about something, and then their true emotions and feelings come out in order to trigger *our* wonder, reflection, and change-agency potential. Plus, how could all of these stories help other students, either individually or collectively as a student body?

The real beauty of storytelling is that it *can* be captured. Stories *can* IGNITE us. But, will we let them IGNITE us or will we walk away forgetting to ask our students what they feel and then fail to use it to drive potential change?

> **Wonder**: Do you wonder if you are missing a good story right now? Will you wonder about what your students are wondering about and ask them to tell you? Then, how will you use what they tell you? Can stories influence students? Can stories influence adults? Can you craft something right now that will begin to work its magic on helping your classroom or school to be even greater than it already is?
>
> **Reflection**: Can you go back to your classroom or school and ask a student to tell you what he or she thinks about a particular problem that you are trying to solve? Can you open up to your students and even share some of what you think are tough adult problems that you are tackling – problems that you think you need to handle alone without your students – but could really use the help of your students and their perceptions to move you forward with fresh, innovative minds and thoughts? Can you think of your students as more mature stakeholders in the community, at large, not just classroom helpers, which localizes their existence?
>
> **Change**: There could be some solutions or powerful stories to get you to arrive at some solutions waiting right around the corner for you. Go ahead and narrativize them. Go ahead and share them.
>> *Can you begin playing with stories right now?*
>> *Can you begin a narrative epidemic?*
>> *Can you stir up passion and create wonder and reflection starting right at this very moment?*
>> *What do you have to lose?*
>> **I wonder.**

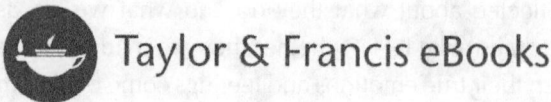 Taylor & Francis eBooks

Helping you to choose the right eBooks for your Library

Add Routledge titles to your library's digital collection today. Taylor and Francis ebooks contains over 50,000 titles in the Humanities, Social Sciences, Behavioural Sciences, Built Environment and Law.

Choose from a range of subject packages or create your own!

Benefits for you
- Free MARC records
- COUNTER-compliant usage statistics
- Flexible purchase and pricing options
- All titles DRM-free.

Benefits for your user
- Off-site, anytime access via Athens or referring URL
- Print or copy pages or chapters
- Full content search
- Bookmark, highlight and annotate text
- Access to thousands of pages of quality research at the click of a button.

 REQUEST YOUR FREE INSTITUTIONAL TRIAL TODAY

Free Trials Available
We offer free trials to qualifying academic, corporate and government customers.

eCollections – Choose from over 30 subject eCollections, including:

Archaeology	Language Learning
Architecture	Law
Asian Studies	Literature
Business & Management	Media & Communication
Classical Studies	Middle East Studies
Construction	Music
Creative & Media Arts	Philosophy
Criminology & Criminal Justice	Planning
Economics	Politics
Education	Psychology & Mental Health
Energy	Religion
Engineering	Security
English Language & Linguistics	Social Work
Environment & Sustainability	Sociology
Geography	Sport
Health Studies	Theatre & Performance
History	Tourism, Hospitality & Events

For more information, pricing enquiries or to order a free trial, please contact your local sales team:
www.tandfebooks.com/page/sales

 Routledge
Taylor & Francis Group

The home of Routledge books

www.tandfebooks.com